Good Manners are Contagious™

The New Rules!

To: Ferdaubah School
Elementary School!
Respect Rooms!
Lori Weiner

Enjoy the read!
Dr. Jodi Stoner

Dr. Jodi Stoner
Lori Weiner

Handbook on Manners/Etiquette, Social Skills Training, and Parenting

At the time of this book's publication, all facts and figures are the most current available; all telephone numbers, addresses, and Web site URLs are accurate and active; all publications, organizations, Web sites, and other resources exist as described in this book; and all have been verified as of April 2009. The authors and Spinner Press make no warranty or guarantee concerning the information and materials given out by organizations or content found at Web sites, and we are not responsible for any changes that occur after this book's publication. To all parents, teachers, and other adults, we strongly urge you to monitor how children use the Internet.

Publishers Note: *Good Manners are Contagious* is designed to provide information to our readers. Neither the author nor the publisher is rendering psychological or medical advice. No warranties or guarantees are expressed or implied by the publisher's decision to include content in this book. Neither the author nor the publisher shall be liable for any psychological, emotional, or physical damages. The *Good Manners are Contagious* Mission Statement provides that individuals are accountable for their own decisions and choices.

All references for factual sources can be found at
www.goodmannersarecontagious.com

Illustrations by Cynthia Foster
Cover Design by Denise Cocha

Special Dedication to Ida Lax— The Mistress of Manners

Our etiquette and elocution inspiration, Ida Lax, was the catalyst for writing this book. Her unending knowledge, unlimited insight, and unrivaled commitment to living a life filled with good manners has had a tremendous influence on us, our families, and what we have achieved personally and professionally throughout our lives.

Thank you, Ida. We are so very grateful for all you have taught us!

Jodi & Lori

ACKNOWLEDGMENTS

We are grateful to so many people who have influenced and encouraged us to respect the value of good manners. Our mothers, Helen Stoner Gordon and Ruby Spinadel Soloff, appreciated the significance of proper etiquette. They provided the essential resource for professional "elocution" lessons, and we were the beneficiaries of a lifetime of social skills and confidence.

In loving memory we acknowledge our fathers Ted Spinadel, Sam Soloff, and Lou Stoner who were invaluable role models. Our grandmothers, Sadie Schiff and Esther Spinadel, were first-generation Americans who pursued the American dream. Our godmother, Beverlee Soloff Shere, has always been a constant source of support, and encouragement.

Many thanks to Lori's husband, Ted, for his love, support, and unwavering confidence.

We are lucky and grateful for the love of our wonderful adult children—TJ, Randi, Lee, and Lonny.

To Cyndi Foster—She brought our book to life with her incredible illustrations.

Many thanks to Larry Gotterer—A master of creative intelligence and an authentic visionary with cutting edge sophistication; a man who is sui generis.

To Dr. Tom Moskowitz for his amazing editing and commitment to our project.

Photography by Clay Wieland, a great guy and a master behind the lens.

A special thanks to Vera Design for their collaborative effort in the design of our logo.

Many thanks to our Web site designer, Larry Argabright from Data Jugglers Computing, Inc.

We give thanks and are so grateful to Josh Rubin—A master at connecting the dots.

To the staff at the Colony Hotel and Cabana Club in Delray Beach, Florida, and Broward County Library, Fort Lauderdale, who provided the highest level of customer service.

Thank you to our inner circle of friends: Marla Appel, Melanie Cohen, Barbara Courshon, Sugar Firtel, Ronni Julien, Elizabeth Mechanic, Eleanor Miller, Dr. Tom Moskowitz, Marcia Rabinowitz, Beverlee Shere, Dr. and Mrs. Sam Steiner, Marsha Sussman, Sheila Wohl, and Sonya Zukerman.

Our thanks to Claire Holloway, Shelley Sapyta, and Cheryl Eichel at BookMasters, Inc. for going over and beyond what any authors could expect.

GET TO KNOW US

Jodi and Lori have extensive experience in the areas of human relations and training in social skills development.

Dr. Jodi Stoner holds a Ph.D. in clinical psychology and is a practicing licensed Mental Health Counselor. She has worked for over 30 years with families, individuals, and couples in parenting, psychotherapy, and life transitions. Dr. Stoner is also an educational specialist with a master's degree in behavior disorders and practiced in the Georgia and Florida public school systems for 15 years. Doc Jodi has served as an expert witness in civil matters. She has been a guest lecturer and high school commencement speaker and has spoken on social skills training, enhancement of self-esteem, and parenting skills training.

Ms. Lori Weiner is a Career Coach with more than 25 years experience as a Career Services Director. While working for Computer Learning Centers, Inc. as National Director of Career Services, Lori oversaw twenty-seven schools nationwide and wrote the *Career Services Training Manual* and other documents covering best practices in the career services field. She has also supervised customer service training at various corporations. Coach Lori has been awarded numerous performance awards, and in 2003 was a speaker at the Florida Association of Postsecondary Schools & Colleges Conference in Orlando, Florida. She continues to mentor new graduates in career development.

On a Personal Note

We are first cousins by birth and best friends by choice. We grew up in an era when manners and civility were expected. These values were supported in the community through civic involvement and television shows that promoted positive interactions in the home. We were also privileged to receive private etiquette and elocution lessons for a combined 11 years. Each of us is proud to have raised two grown children and we can attest that we survived the "terrible twos" and "challenging teens," and you will, too!

We want to share our experiences with you so that you pass them on to your children so they will grow up like ours—confident, courteous and successful. Please share your experiences with us on our Web site at www.goodmannersarecontagious.com

WHY YOU SHOULD Spread the Word!

Why Spread the Word?

We have all said to ourselves, "the world would be a better place if people were more respectful." It begins with one person at a time. The investment you make in teaching your child good manners creates a family legacy that lasts a lifetime. The "New Rules" for instilling good manners are timely and imperative. Once these New Rules become ingrained—intentional acts of respectfulness, kindness, and caring are passed on to others.

How to Spread the Word?

Be an architect for change. Passing it on begins with personal accountability. With that comes the responsibility for "doing the right thing" and respecting others' acts of kindness. Acts of respect are recognized and reinforced by your family, your community, and the world. Raising social awareness is pivotal for positive change in a civilized world. Inspiring others to make a difference creates the ripple effect that energizes change.

What Is the Message?

To raise social awareness.

Reinforce the message by wearing Good Manners wristbands and giving them to others, along with Good Manners stickers, when you witness acts of kindness and respect.

Take the challenge and tap into your human spirit. The benefits are endless, beginning with feeling good about yourself.

Please visit us at www.goodmannersarecontagious.com. Let's work together to give our world a much needed manners makeover!

Good Manners Are Contagious

Start a New Chapter in Your Family's Life ... and Save Your Sanity!

InTRodUCtiON

Why this book about manners, and why NOW?

For a so-called civilized society, isn't it amazing how uncivilized people can be? Sometimes it just seems like the entire world is out of control. Like now.

We have been bombarded with news reports of bad manners in every aspect of our society. Front page stories and media frenzy have exposed movie stars, heiresses, shock jocks, runway models, and sports heroes exhibiting obnoxious behavior. From seriously corrupt government officials to celebrity wardrobe malfunctions, our society is

on a collision course with social disaster! Sex bands, anorexic heroines, shameless reality shows—and the end is not in sight! Recent news stories tell of teenagers arrested for "sexting," and these arrest violations will stay in their record forever.

Offensive conduct affects everyone, but few people bother to do anything about it or just feel helpless, shake their heads in disgust, and try not to let it get to them—but eventually it *does* get to them. Bad manners have no socioeconomic boundaries and they affect every aspect of your child's life.

Circus-like behavior has left the Big Top and spilled into our neighborhoods. Have you ever been in a restaurant and seen a swarm of children running around as if they were on a playground? "Where are the parents," you ask? Why, they are sitting at the table, pretending it is someone else's responsibility to monitor their children's behavior.

Remember your last air travel experience? Toddlers running up and down the aisles. Next, the attendants try to serve refreshments but cannot because PARENTS let their children run amok. Are you pulling your hair out yet?

These rude and obnoxious children and their parents were not born this way. Years of ineffective training, or no training at all, created these poorly mannered people we encounter in our lives every day.

Internet bloggers, who happen to be parents, even have "anti-kid" campaigns running on various Web sites, with some bloggers asserting that mealtime with dogs is preferable to mealtime with children!

Are you crazed with the present condition of our society and truthfully, isn't it getting worse? Are you appalled at the countless number of disrespectful and inconsiderate people everywhere? If you are sick and tired of this, then this is your opportunity to jump in and raise the bar to a new level of social consciousness!

Now would be a great time to look in the mirror. Really—go to the mirror, look yourself right in the eye, and ask: What kind of manners does my family have?

Parents have become increasingly frustrated in their efforts to raise a well-mannered and well-grounded child in today's perpetually disrespectful world. However, as a parent, it is your *moral obligation* to teach your children the skills needed to live and succeed in our challenging society. It is never too late to embrace change, and to pass it on! So think of this book as a reality check for you and a survival guide for your children.

Facts of the Manner:

88% of people with or without children agree that the failure to instill behavior is the major cause of bad manners.
– *U.S. News and World Report* study

84% of people see others as rude and disrespectful.
– ABC News *20/20* survey

93% of people felt that an increasingly rude society was the result of parents' failure to stress the importance of good manners and a tendency to overlook bad behavior.
– Associated Press Poll

88% of adults felt that incivility is a serious problem and getting worse.
– Penn State University National Poll

70% of kids say disrespectful behavior is common in their schools.
– *USA Today*

CHAPTER ONE

THE NEW RULES

The family unit is the core foundation of your home. Parents are the architects that build this foundation. In the process, you are also building a stronger family unit. Whether you're a couple about to have a new child, or you already have children, or you're a single parent trying to get a handle on things, creating a Blueprint for Living and learning the "New Rules" will give you the tools needed to create this foundation.

Parents must implement same-page thinking regarding children's manners. This means that parents agree to provide positive and consistent training. This consistency creates a roadmap of civility for the family, home, school, community, and society.

The New Rules for Your Family's Blueprint for Living:

Create Strong Family Values
Integrate these values:
Honesty, integrity, generosity, caring, tolerance, conservation, and respect for our planet into everyday life and live by them.

Design Effective Channels of Communication: Establish positive, ongoing, and open dialogue with family members:

- **Teach** children how to show love and respect in all dialogue, especially during disagreements. Yelling at each other never works because everyone shuts down.
- **Create** boundaries, which means no damaging personal attacks or physical violence, EVER!
- **Forgiveness** is essential to reconnect to family members, and don't harbor a grudge—life is too short!

Structure Family Expectations and Goals:

- A goal is an accomplishment, something that you want to achieve. A goal can be getting better grades or saving for a computer.
- Setting goals with your child will make him feel good about himself. This is an important life skill that children need for the rest of their lives.

Teach your child about goals:

- Initially discuss goals and expectations with your partner.
- Introduce the concept of "why" and "how" to your child in a fun way.
- Make the goal simple, specific, attainable, and timely.

An important value to teach your child is how to communicate effectively. Children must learn the fine art of compromise, problem solving, and conflict resolution.

—Doc Jodi

> **Example Goal:**
> **Spend more family time together:**
> 1. Start with one night a week when all family members have no other activity.
> 2. Children must finish homework after school and adult chores are completed.
> 3. Family meets together in family room for 30 minutes before bed time.
> 4. Each week a different family member chooses the activity for the 30-minute meeting.

Good manners afford our children a lifetime of benefits, which paves the way for future success. Learning proper protocol is a pivotal component of one's personal, social, and business success.

Learning socially correct behavior, i.e., good manners, offers a child invaluable life skills. The benefits of developing these life skills contribute to the growth and expression of a child's sense of self-worth and self-esteem. These are core values in one's development. On the other hand, self-absorption or self-interest is both limiting and self-serving.

It seems like society has either forgotten, become immune to, or just takes for granted the great, classic Golden Rule: DO UNTO OTHERS. Here's a New Golden Rule to live by:

Using proper manners and demonstrating empathy becomes an inherent way of responding to others. You no longer have to *think* about responding kindly; you simply *do* respond kindly.

Good Manners Are Contagious

Rate your parent–child relationship—you might be surprised at your answers.

Quick Quiz

1. Do your children scream at you?

2. Do your children witness disrespectful family interactions?

3. Do you get negative feedback from teachers at school?

4. Do parents complain about your child after play dates?

5. Are you disappointed by the way your child behaves in public places?

6. Does your child get everything she wants?

7. Do you find yourself making excuses for your child?

8. Is your child involved in questionable Internet activities?

9. Are you losing control in front of your child more often than ever?

10. Has your child been a bully or been bullied at school?

1 to 3 "Yes" Answers: You're ahead of the game, so use this book to reinforce the positive messages you've been preaching.

4 to 6 "Yes" Answers: It's not too late to take control back and turn things around for your sake, the sake of others, and the benefit of your child.

7 or more "Yes" Answers: Sounds like you've got your *hands full*. Keep reading and learning as fast as you can!

If your answers to these questions give you reason to *pause*, perhaps

This is your "Ah-Ha Moment."

In the following chapters, you will learn how to give your children a Manners Makeover.

CHAPTER TWO

SELF-ESTEEM MAKES KIDS BEAM

Well-Rounded Starts With Well-Grounded

True life success is defined by the combination of three key ingredients: healthy self-esteem, good manners, and mastered life skills.

Self-esteem is how one feels about oneself. It starts in the home. The greatest gift you can give your child is for her to feel, "I am of value." Children must always feel loved, accepted, and respected.

A child's interpretation of whether he is loved or unloved will affect his emotional growth and development for the rest of his life. The message must be: **Love your child** for *who* he is rather than *what* he does.

Tip: Disparaging nicknames like "Porky" or "Nimrod" can have a lifelong damaging effect on your child's self-esteem.

Children often tell me that they feel unloved. This perception is derived from feeling that their parents are too busy to make enough time for critical connections. It doesn't have to be all or nothing—quality time always supersedes quantity time.

—Doc Jodi

11

Kick Start Your Child's Self-Esteem

Raise the praise: Tell your child every day how worthwhile he is and how much he is loved.

Try VIP treatment: Enjoy your child every day and find ways to make him feel unique and special.

Focus on fairness: Discipline with respect and kindness.

Cut some slack: Allow your child to make mistakes and teach forgiveness.

Side with pride: Teach children to respect and protect their bodies.

Review "their" view: Respect your child's opinion without necessarily embracing it.

Include your dude (or dudette): Involve your child in daily activities to build self-esteem.

Positive Manner Moment: "Sammy, thank you so much for helping mommy with the baby. You are such a helpful big brother!"

Negative Manner Moment: "Sammy, don't bother me when I am changing the baby!"

Successful interpersonal relationships can only occur when we feel good about ourselves. When self-esteem begins in the home and is fostered at school, it paves the way for healthy personal and professional relationships.
—Doc Jodi

My mother-in-law used to say, "You get back from children what you put in." Children thrive in a loving, caring, and mutually respectful household.
—Coach Lori

A child with good manners shines like a bright star. These children clearly stand apart from others, and these qualities are apparent to all.

 Tip: Parents will get better feedback from their child when they say, "It looks like you had a great day today," rather than the standard, "How was your day today?" Then, **just listen**.

Reflect this!
"Looks like it was a difficult day."
"You seem tired today."
"It's so nice to see you happy."
"I saw you walking out with Kendra today. It must feel good to be friends again."

Your child will shine and receive straight A's in manners management when they:

Achieve: Share school accomplishments
Adapt: Get along with peer groups
Accept: Respect others
Adjust: Stay open and comfortable with others
Apply: Interact well with adults
Absorb: Know when to enter the conversation

The first five minutes that you share with your child after school is a critical window of opportunity for embracing dialogue with your child.
—Coach Lori

Good Manners Attract the Right Kind of Attention

Good-mannered children are attractive and popular with others. Kind, courteous, and respectful behavior is appealing. Children love to please, so show yours how positive manner moments can be contagious!

Go Ahead, Make Someone's Day ...

Monday: Let a person with one item go ahead of you in line to check out.

Tuesday: Pay for another person in line if they are missing small change.

Wednesday: Volunteer with your child to help an elderly or disabled neighbor with chores.

Thursday: Put a kindness note in your child's lunch box.

Friday: Compliment a stranger and make them feel good.

Saturday: Hold the door open for someone right behind you.

Sunday: Put your shopping cart in its rightful place in or out of the store.

Monday: Let the car in the next lane into your lane instead of racing ahead to prevent it.

Tuesday: Gather up all used toys and take them to a hospital or children's center.

Wednesday: Show your child that people matter, not "things".

Thursday: Your turn to think of some memorable manner moments to try.

<u>You</u> are your child's most important life coach. Children reflect your values learned in the home. Parents must listen, encourage, and inspire their children to achieve a purposeful life. Teach your child to empathize with other's needs, even before his own.

—Coach Lori

Making Impressive Impressions

What Language Does Your Body Speak?

Your body language speaks volumes to others. Body language is a silent yet powerful form of communication. Children are very savvy when it comes to reading a parent's body language, so be aware of how they perceive you. Sending mixed messages between body language and verbal messages are confusing to your child. Send the right signals and be consistent with what you say and your facial/body expressions.

A good first impression takes only a few moments to make but lasts a lifetime. Good manners are like education; no one can ever take them away from you! Once learned, manners become ingrained and automatic.

Recently, a mother came into the office concerned about her 13-year-old daughter's misconduct at school. The child had alienated most of her friends with her provocative dress. When asked why she allowed her daughter to dress that way, the mother replied, "I can't stop her." In a parent's effort to be "cool," many give in and promote inappropriate behavior without thinking of consequences. Too much, too soon is not the answer.
—Doc Jodi

Your son will make an outstanding first impression if he is dressed appropriately and shows confidence when interviewing for college admissions, a job interview, or attending a special occasion/event.
—Coach Lori

Learn the Right Moves

Straighten-Up: Good posture shows poise.
Hands-Out: A firm handshake shows self-assurance and self-confidence.
Make Contact: Eye contact gets others' attention and lets them know you are listening.
Eye Straight Ahead: Avoid rolling your eyes—an undisputed sign of disrespect.
Express Yourself: Facial expressions are an interpretation of emotion.
Face Facts: Learn to read facial expressions and become aware of your own.

 Tip: Chewing gum is acceptable as long as others cannot hear it—snapping, cracking, and popping translates to annoying, aggravating, and irritating.

 Tip: Always cover your mouth when you yawn. Other than your dentist, how many people want to see a close-up of your tonsils?

Example: What does your body language say when your least favorite aunt comes to visit? Your body language emits one signal, your actions another. Not only will your aunt sense your poor disposition, but your child will pick up mixed messages. More importantly, it does not allow for your child to decide for herself how she feels about your aunt.

17

Dressing Up Your Manners

Aren't you tired of the screaming and tantrums over your kids' skimpy or slovenly clothes? Have you ever stopped to think how your child is perceived by others? Mini-me dressing is simply not appropriate for children. Trouble is looming when children 5 years old dress like they're 22! They become "sexualized" and may feel compelled to act out.

Encouraging children to wear makeup and jewelry that doesn't fit their developmental age is an accident waiting to happen. In the quest to raise "cool kids," parents host seemingly benign birthday parties that encourage makeovers, massages, and other adult pleasures, which contribute to this delinquency.

Use Your Parent Power

One of the biggest causes of family arguments is agreeing on appropriate clothing. How do you change her mind without starting a family war? The point is this—you *cannot* and *must not* give in! Peer pressure is powerful, but so is teaching self-respect. It's essential to communicate acceptable choices using positive ongoing dialogue. Praise your child when she does choose appropriate clothing for the occasion.

Be Clothes Minded: Give children acceptable choices for clothing; ultimately you are the one buying it.

Use Your Dress Code: Explain to your children why certain clothing is NOT acceptable, such as bratty and trashy slogans on T-shirts.

Diffuse Tantrums by Accessorizing: Suggest a closet alteration, different hair ornaments, change of hair style, shoes makeover, etc.

Tip: Halloween is not a license to allow your child to dress provocatively. Stick with the holiday theme—scary or silly, not sexy.

Tweens are influenced by their parents, peers, and the media. Because they often struggle with their own identity and personal choices, parents MUST stay connected to their child's world inside and outside of the home. Read their books, watch their movies, listen to their music, and surf their Web sites.
—Doc Jodi

Prevent nagging later in life by explaining to young children that there is a time and place for everything—jeans and a sweatshirt included. Give direction and suggestions with respect to clothing that is acceptable for an event and allow your child to choose his outfit within those guidelines.
—Coach Lori

CHAPTER THREE

THE PARENT CONNECTION-CORRECTION

How to Counter: "Who Cares?"… "So What!"… and "Why Bother?"

Once upon a time, value was placed on the importance of proper social graces. It was *expected* that children do the right thing. There were no parent–child negotiations. Back then, the world was clearly a kinder, gentler place. In the typical household, one adult left the home daily to work. Mom was at home baking cookies and waiting for the kids to come home from school. Today, in most households, both parents work. They come home from work tired and complain of too little time, physical exhaustion, pressure at work—and the list goes on and on. These issues aside, the parental responsibility remains: **You must make time to prioritize the importance of teaching respect and good manners.**

Teaching good manners creates a family legacy that your children will pass on. Parental direction and correction steer your child toward a future path for success and competencies in the real world. One of the most essential lessons a parent can impart to her child is the concept of being grateful. Parents want their children to succeed in the world with self-esteem, self-awareness, and proper protocol. The only way your child will learn your values is by watching you embrace them.

The Value of Values

The Blueprint for Living defines your
family's integrity. Honesty, empathy,
respect, and responsibility are values
that must be taught. It is never too early
(or late) to teach family values.

Values learned at home are best incorporated in selfless acts
of kindness. When children participate in your good deeds,
they do their own good deeds. Additionally, communicating
why we employ these behaviors reinforces the message.
Plan family projects that help others who are less fortunate.

**The best way for your children to learn your value system is
by living it.**

DEVELOP your child's character (actions speak louder than words).
CONNECT to your children through active listening,
communicating, and special alone time.
DELEGATE specific responsibilities for each family member.
FOSTER personal accountability with: "Own it, admit it, and move
on from it."

*Be conscious of being grateful. Teach your children to be grateful by being
thankful. For example, choose a family night dinner and ask each family
member to verbalize what he or she is grateful for and why. Gratefulness is
contagious, and family members will learn how to appreciate each other.*

—Coach Lori

Don't Pass the Buck

In these volatile economic times, it is essential to teach children respect for the dollar. This must start at a young age and they must be taught the difference between *wants* and *needs*.

Developing Manners that are Right on the Money

Pre-School Age (2–5)
Begin by putting pennies in a piggybank.
Introduce the concept of an allowance for doing extra chores.
Teach your child how to compare prices in a store.
Teach this concept: "Today we will be looking, not buying."

Older Children (6–9)
When dining out, discuss menu prices.
The purpose of an allowance should be for saving and buying their own extras.
Have your child contribute to big-ticket items with her allowance.

Bank of
Mom & Dad

> **Example:** Designate one family meeting to discuss family finances: "The money we make by working pays for our rent/mortgage, car, food, clothes, phone, and entertainment." This is the first essential introduction to money management.

When children are given toys and gifts indiscriminately on a regular basis, the message is "I am entitled to everything all the time." This sets your child up for future failure and disappointment.

—*Doc Jodi and Coach Lori*

Does Your Child Suffer From "Affluenza?"

How do you know if you are giving your children "too much?" Does your child have every "i-THING" there is? Are your children blatantly ungracious and blasé when they receive a generous gift? Many children feel entitled to live a life of affluence, while their parents are living paycheck to paycheck. Well, that's what we call "Affluenza"— the desire for things without either an appreciation for the item, what it cost, or what sacrifice was made to get it. Most children of the Excess Generation get too much too soon, and are not told "No" enough.

> **Example:** Byron is a single dad who works in a nearby office. His paycheck barely makes ends meet. Yet his teenage son proudly shows off the hottest phone, ridiculously expensive sneakers, and a fully loaded laptop. Clearly, this parent is sending the wrong message with monetary overindulgence.

It's not what you can afford or want to buy your child; irresponsible spending sends out a disturbing message that counteracts the real needs of the child.
                                                            —Doc Jodi

Your child is overindulged if he or she:

- Is dependent
- Is irresponsible
- Is unable to delay gratification
- Generalizes failure in one area to failure in all areas
- Does not feel competent
- Has difficulty making a decision
- Wears you down until you give in

How to avoid overindulgence:

> **"No, means no!"**—Set limits and boundaries.
> **Create a "To-Do" list**—Make chores a routine way of life.
> **"You'll have to earn it."**—Introduce money management.
> **"Why do you need it?"**—Help your child differentiate between wants and needs.
> **"Well done, Bravo!"**—Reward your child with non-monetary items such as a hug and time alone with you.

Tip: Introduce the concept of stating the boundary **once only**—repetitive reminders only lead to nagging.

Self-indulgence undermines a child's self-confidence and creates a false sense of entitlement. Keep your child's expectations down to earth.
—Doc Jodi

Extravagant nurturing results in the "my child can do no wrong" syndrome. This trend is not limited to any socioeconomic group. Overindulgence is the hallmark of "helicopter parents," who incessantly hover over their child. Parents do homework, create school excuses, sweep up after, and deny their children the skills needed to achieve independence. Furthermore, these children are deprived of the opportunity to develop into personally accountable adults. Parents can remedy this by setting family and individual goals and creating designated family time.

Parent Correction

You've Made the Connection, Now Make the Correction

Clues for Sending the Proper Cues

Harness the power of communication with your child through nonverbal cues. A nonverbal cue is a signal to let her know what is expected of her. Using a cue eliminates the need to scream, shout, or embarrass your child. Parents can teach this skill with sign language, gestures, and facial expressions. Design your own cryptic or discreet dialogue between you and your child. These are our favorites:

Use hand movements such as a to indicate "shhhh."

Try eye movements such as a or a certain blink to convey "do the right thing."

Whisper or sign the letter " " to say "calm down."

Hold your  up close to your shoulder to signal "stop."

Using cues in public places is much more effective than raising your voice. The calmer you remain, the better your child will respond. Try it—it works!
—Coach Lori

Are you ready to use what you've learned to gain more control with love and boundaries? Here is a No-Holding-Back Action Plan to get you started:

NON-NEGOTIABLE MANNER MANDATES

1. YOU need to take charge. Nip a tantrum in the bud. Let your child know the rules and stick to them. Parents must stay calm and *never* bribe your child.

2. "I am the parent and you are the child." Say it with love, and mean it!

3. Don't be afraid to say "No." Giving in is not easier. Consistency with your partner is imperative. Think bigger picture!

4. Become morally empowered to teach empathy. Your child maybe the center of your world, but the world does not revolve around him.

5. Children are your children until they become adults; only then can they become your "friends." Your primary role is that of parent, period.

CHAPTER FOUR

BABY STEPS 101

The Real Work Starts After Labor

Wouldn't it be nice if all babies came with an owner's manual?

Under the best of circumstances, having a new baby is overwhelming. No matter how prepared you think you are, finding time for yourself does become a daunting task. Time management is essential.

These helpful hints will ease your transition into parenthood:

Why be a martyr? Delegate responsibilities. Recruit help.
What about tomorrow? Plan in advance for the expected and unexpected. Lay everything out the night before for yourself and your baby for the next day. Prepare ahead of time and post a coordinated schedule.
Enjoy your new running partner. Exercise, take your baby out and go!
Baby yourself, too. Nurture yourself; nap when the baby naps; pamper yourself with a new hairdo or manicure.
Need a support group? Ask others to help; start a neighborhood play group with other new parents. In a pinch, you can all benefit by babysitting.
What to do, to do, to do? Set and list your priorities in order of importance. Use time effectively by banking by mail; use cleaners that pick up at your home, other home services, etc.
NOW is the time. Attend to the basics; stay focused in the "now," not what has to be done next week.
It's all within reach. Organize space in your home for all necessary baby items.

Baby See, Baby Do

Babies mimic adults and react to their parents. Thus begins the concept of setting limits. Start off modeling the very actions you want your baby to learn. You aren't verbally teaching them, but actively showing them. This is a parent's first connection with their baby for teaching trust, which is the beginning of respect. Although your baby may still be in your arms, showing politeness to others becomes her first observed social interaction.

Keep Cool: Make corrections and suggestions kindly.
Keep Calm: Respond to babies tenderly.
Keep in Touch: Use simple gestures to teach please and thank you.

Babies cry when they are hungry, wet, or tired. Make certain your baby is fed, diapered, and rested before you leave the house. Your baby is too young to have manners, so that means it's all up to you to do the right thing around other people.

Tip: No one wants to listen to your screaming baby in a public place. If your child is wailing in any public place, you need to pick up your baby and leave the room.

Manners that considerate and prepared parents pick up are:

Keep Abreast of Feeding-Time Manners—Nurse babies in a comfortable and discreet place.
Don't Make a Stink about Cleaning-Up Manners—Carry plastic bags to dispose of dirty diapers.
Get to the Bottom-of-Things Manners—Always carry a diaper pad - no one wants you to use their rug.
Time for Some Peace-and-Quiet Manners—Set aside time for naps.

When traveling with your infant, plan flight times to coincide with nap time. Mornings or evenings are usually the best times for infant travel. Most airlines will pre-board, but don't expect the airlines to provide infant necessities. Always remember to respect others on the flight.
—Coach Lori

 Tip: Be considerate. Oversized jogging strollers, car seats, pet strollers and other personal accessories get in the way of others. It would be great if "Bugaboo Valets" existed, but they don't, so it's your responsibility.

CHAPTER FIVE

TODDLER TROUBLES

Experts in child rearing believe that we can teach our children basic principles of etiquette as early as six months of age. In fact, from the moment your baby is born, your child is developing his sense of self and self-worth.

Teaching good manners to toddlers requires consistency and **constant repetition**. This is an age of exploration and testing limits. When introducing manners to toddlers you are creating the foundation for polite behavior. Don't underestimate your toddler's abilities. Toddlers love to mimic others and are little sponges with what they see and hear. Make certain the examples you set emphasize the right message.

Social niceties are taught in the moment.

- ✓ Saying hello
- ✓ Shaking hands when prompted
- ✓ Respecting the word "No!"
- ✓ Cover mouth when sneezing and yawning
- ✓ Not picking your nose in public
- ✓ Keeping your hands out of your pants
- ✓ Stepping out of the room to pass gas

> **Example:** Keri, age 1, pointed to an apple and said, "Gimmee."
> Mom corrected her by saying, "Say please, Keri."

Tip: Toddlers thrive on routine. Routine provides reassurance, consistency, and security.

You would be amazed how many preschool teachers are appalled by the poor manners they see every day in the classroom. Shoving, bullying, and using foul language may seem cute to you at four, but if unchecked will not be better at fifteen. These are the formative years— make sure your child is a kind kid in training.

—Coach Lori

TERRIFIC TODDLER TIPS

Tame toddler troubles with these terrific tips...

Your new secret weapon—Consistency; it's the key to keeping kids in line.

Breathe in, breathe out—You can learn to stay calm, but you'll have to practice doing it first.

Don't get sucked in—Never giving in to a tantrum.

Say it, mean it—Mean the word "No" when you say it.

Who's in charge here anyway? Give direct and clear instructions of what's expected.

Hey, look at that! Point out when other children are using good manners.

Is there a helper in the house? Encourage your child to do small tasks or chores.

Get in the Good Manners mindset—Read books that teach your child about sharing, fair play, and other good etiquette skills.

Making mornings manageable is simply, well, magical. Here's how...

> **Ready...set...snuggle**—Start your day with a hug—it's worth the extra time!
>
> **Digest this**—Attitude is everything so set a calm and positive tone for the day.
>
> **Prepare for liftoff**—Set out clothes and lay out breakfast the night before.
>
> **Be the leader of the pack**—Pack snacks and lunches together the night before.

Toddlers love to have fun—don't you? A great approach for teaching manners is by creating fun, rhyming songs or sentences that integrate manners into everyday life. For instance, "Can Jillian pass the cheese, please, and does she cover her mouth when she sneezes?"

—Coach Lori

Reinforce the MAGIC WORDS:

"Please"

"Thank you"

"You're welcome"

"Excuse me"

"I'm sorry"

Turn Down the Volume

It is not okay for children to "express themselves" at any time or any place, with little regard for the consideration of others. When children

are loud or rude, don't miss the opportunity to teach them the importance of **"the quiet voice"** or **"inside voice."** Children listen better when they feel respected rather than attacked. Toddlers learn positive and negative voice tone from their parents. It's not always what you say; very often it's *how* you say it.

Watch your tone—Use quiet voices in confined places such as the movies, restaurants, library, airplanes, etc.
Adjust the volume—Redirect your child's pitch by whispering yourself.
Save your breath—Use the calm breathing technique described below to restore calm.
Be handy—Try a hand signal as a cue to settle your child down.

Calm Breathing Technique: Teach your child to calm down by using the calm breathing technique. Using a bottle of bubbles, hold the wand in front of your mouth and take a deep breath in and then slowly blow out the bubble. The emphasis is on control. This method will reinforce your child's ability to go from a screaming voice to a *quiet voice* by pretending he is blowing bubbles in a calm and deliberate way.

Conversation Interrupt-Us

Interrupting is a bad habit that is difficult to break. Many children, and even adults, are self-centered and don't understand, or even take into consideration the needs of

others. Most children seek immediate attention/gratification,

especially when a parent is engaged in conversation. Training children

not to interrupt teaches them patience and how to wait their turn.

Frequent use of the phrase "Excuse me" is not a license to interrupt

freely and continuously. Toleration of this by parents is annoying to

everyone!

How do you go from "DON'T INTERRUPT!" without having to yell "SHUT UP?"

Think quickly—Young toddlers need a quick response time.
Take pause—Say, "I'll be with you in a moment" in a calm voice.
Learn a new language—Teach young children to read simple sign language cues.
Toy with your child—Put a box of toys near the phone to keep your child occupied.
Give yourself a time out—Prepare your child ahead of time if you are expecting company and let him know that you need adult time.

To Interrupt or Not to Interrupt—WHEN is the question?

Teach your child what constitutes rightful interruption. This should be a pressing or critical situation such as:

Emergencies—Someone is hurt
Urgencies—Bathroom runs or someone at the door

To coach assertiveness and self-esteem, teach your child to let the cashier know he was passed over while waiting in line. It's alright to politely say to the cashier, "Excuse me, but I think I was next."

—Coach Lori

TABLE MANNER MISHAPS

A child of three or older should be able to sit at a table for at least 15 minutes. A young child is going to be messy, so plan ahead with a piece of plastic under a highchair or dining chair. If you are going out to dinner, bring a small toy or several crayons and a piece of paper to keep your child occupied.

At the table, teach your child to:

Use the "Magic Words."

Table the television—Engage in conversation with the TV off.

Avoid the "break" dance—Use a non-breakable plate and child-sized spoon and fork.

Size up the food—Cut up food in bite-size portions.

Skip the cow impersonation—Chew quietly and with the mouth closed.

Wait for your cue—Sit at the table until excused.

Yum Yum
Thanks For the
Grub

Tip: If your child does not want to eat, don't force her. Instruct her that, "No, thank you" is the correct response.

Forcing children to eat and making a big deal over food (hiding snacks, having a clean plate) has a direct relationship to future eating disorders. Emotional attachment to food should be kept to a minimum.

—Doc Jodi

Safe Proof Your Child

Teach your child:

- ✓ Never talk to strangers.
- ✓ If you see a gun, NEVER touch it.
- ✓ Never get into a car with people you don't know.
- ✓ The physical boundaries where your child is allowed to roam in the neighborhood.
- ✓ To run if they feel threatened.
- ✓ A procedure to use if they feel threatened—and review regularly.
- ✓ Not to ride their bikes alone and not to take shortcuts through fields or alleys.
- ✓ Always look both ways before crossing the road.
- ✓ Not to go alone into a public bathroom.
- ✓ What to do when he gets lost.

Safety Tips:

- Your child must know his name and phone number at as young an age as possible.
- Provide your child with an identification card.
- Fingerprint your child.
- Leave a medical alert/release card with whoever is watching him.
- Always carry a recent picture of your child.
- Never leave your child in the car alone even for a second.
- Always buckle your child's seat belt—it's the law.

Check it out:
Did you know there are:

GPS Technologies that track your child's whereabouts with devices that can be worn in wristbands and clothing or placed in book bags.

Nanny Cams will watch over your child when you're not there.

Chapter Six

PERFECTING PLAY

Peers, Play Dates, Playgroups, and Playgrounds

The Peer Factor

Is my child tall enough, smart enough, and popular enough? Many parents worry how their child is perceived by other children.

That is precisely why "play" is so important to a child's confidence and self-worth. Play is the part of friendship that sets the climate for social development. One of the most important elements to note is that children like other children who are mannerly, who don't call others names, who are not bullies, and who are good sports. They have a tendency to gravitate to those children who are beginning to demonstrate the social graces—sharing, caring, belonging, and respect. Initially, it is your responsibility as the parent to find and oversee friendship development.

The decisions that parents make when prioritizing activities for their children can make a difference in social skills maturity. In order of importance, life skills development and cultivating friendships ranks right up there with making good grades.

—Doc Jodi

Be aware that a social hierarchy (cliques) exists even in elementary school. These cliques impact your child's self-esteem. Understand what they are, where your child fits in, and their influence on your child's emotional well-being.

—Coach Lori

The Friendship Connection

- ✓ Make room in your child's schedule to accommodate friendship activities.
- ✓ Ask your child's teacher who your child plays with at school.
- ✓ Make sure new playmates are age appropriate and well-mannered.
- ✓ Connect with other parents in your child's class.
- ✓ Join after-school activities.
- ✓ Join groups like Mommy and Me, Gymboree, and other established parent–child groups.

The Play Date Effect

You've met the parent, now set up the date. Before you begin, role play different social situations with your child, including potential conflicts that

Tip: Excessive time in front of the screen does not provide the skills needed for socialization. Playing sports or board games will provide a solution.

might arise. Make these role-play situations a game and help the child find the desired outcome. Explain along the way how mannerly interactions will enable them to make more friends.

What to Expect:

- ✓ If you call a parent for a play date, you are hosting the date.
- ✓ Pick the time and place.
- ✓ Inform the guest parent where you are going and the duration of the date.
- ✓ For children under 5 years old, the parent accompanies the child and, as the host, you are entertaining the parent, too.
- ✓ Young children often play side by side, not necessarily playing together. It's still a great play date!
- ✓ Plan the play date time to correspond with age.

> **Example:** Sasha, age 10 from Houston, was asked to join a play date with several children while on vacation in Miami. It was apparent from her ease of sharing, cooperating, and respecting others, that she felt comfortable with new friends and had mastered the art of play.

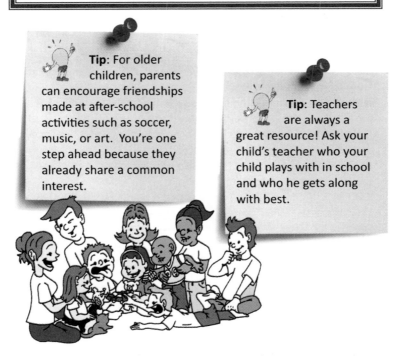

Tip: For older children, parents can encourage friendships made at after-school activities such as soccer, music, or art. You're one step ahead because they already share a common interest.

Tip: Teachers are always a great resource! Ask your child's teacher who your child plays with in school and who he gets along with best.

Children acclimate more successfully in elementary school social situations when they have had previous positive play date encounters. Each play date offers a different experience to practice social skills and gain confidence.
—Coach Lori

The Playgroup Effect

Playgroups help children develop independence and self-confidence.

These small play situations provide an opportunity to model appropriate interactions with small groups of parents and their children. Playgroups are informal and work best when children are close in age. The size of the group should be no more than six children. It is also a great way for parents to support each other, share parenting tips, and enhance business networking.

> **How to start a Playgroup:**
> **HAVE A PLAN**—Invite and discuss with several interested parents how the playgroup will be set up.
> **GROUND RULES**—Discuss common problems and solutions such as biting, sharing, name calling, etc.
> **PLAY TIME**—The younger the children, the smaller the group, the shorter the length time.
> **PARENTS PROSPECTIVE**—Parents should plan to stay with their child.

The Playground Effect

Community and school playgrounds are ideal places to find new friends for your child to play with. Children who have mastered play dates and playgroups will have a smoother transition adapting

to socialization. The rules of playground etiquette—sharing, taking turns, not bullying—apply here as well.   Be creative—bring something from home that other children will want to play with.

Have your child:

Observe others in play before joining in.
Say something positive to another child ("I like your toy.")
Ask to join in—timing is everything!
Respect other's property.

Tip: Encourage your child to show enjoyment with other children and express this in her body language with a smile, posture, and eye contact.

Tip: On the playground, point out children who share their toys, take turns, and include others in group play.

Demonstrate intervention techniques when your child appears angry or frustrated. When he gets angry and lashes out at others, remain calm. Take him aside and make eye contact, "This is not what friends do. Think about how Carly is feeling." If he needs additional time to calm down, go for a walk or sit down on the park bench.

—Doc Jodi

Taking playground politics into consideration, it may be wise to let your child know that she may not be included immediately in group play. It's okay for her to play alone until invited to join in, or have her seek out another child who is playing alone and ask her to play.

—Coach Lori

Chapter Seven

SPORTING GOOD MANNERS

A brawl breaks out between two college football teams on national TV, causing team suspensions. An Olympic skater loses a potential gold medal when she is injured by her rival. A famous tennis player is unashamed as he throws his racquet around time and time again showing poor sportsmanship. Recently, a hockey player deliberately broke the nose of the opposing team's coach. Imagine watching a professional basketball game with your child when the players stop to throw chairs at fans in the stands? Not to mention the ever increasing use of steroids and other illegal performance drugs in sports. Even superstars have lost their medals and have had their past accomplishments questioned. What must our children be thinking and what values are we, and these athletic role models society puts up on a pedestal, passing on to them?

Children that witness disrespect become disrespectful adults. They watch with a vigilant eye how we act and react, and how we handle life's curve balls on and off the field, all the time! There are no Time Outs in parenting.

This book is your "Personal Manners Playbook." Failure to coach your child opens the door for others to coach them, perhaps in ways that don't reflect *your* values. Parents have the tools to connect and correct everyday interpersonal experiences.

Step Up to the Plate!

This should be included in every Parent/Coach Personal Manners Playbook:

Everyone plays—Allow all team members to participate.
Show consideration—Always keep your players focused on fair play.
Halt the heckling—Treat other teams with respect.
Get a grip! Maintain self-control at all times.
No trash talk—Don't shout out messages that are verbally abusive (booing and worse!)
Hold it in—Avoid arguing with an official or referee during the game, even if you don't agree. Take them aside after the game and speak to them in private, preferably not in front of any children, including yours.
Lock your ego in your locker—Don't blame other players if they did not play their best. Everyone is entitled to a "bad day."
Say "NO" to scandal—Whatever you do, discourage falsifying anything or cheating.

Tip: No matter how competitive a game can be, it's always cool to see professional players shake hands after the final buzzer. Make sure to point that out!

The harder you are on your child for losing a sporting event, the worse he will feel when he loses. Participating in a team sport teaches your child the value of teamwork and the value of individual contribution. Feeling a sense of team ownership is what will make your child feel empowered.

The mentality that "winning is everything" is an unfortunate message passed on by misguided adults. The point of playing sports, or any game, is to have a good time. Teach your children how to lose gracefully; sometimes losing can be a winning experience.

Sport friendships that start early in life may last a lifetime. As these friendships continue into adulthood, sport leagues continue to develop character and competitive life skills. This benefit also cultivates business deals and creates new social networking contacts.

—Doc Jodi

Chapter Eight

SINGLE-PARENT SOLUTIONS

According to the 2007 U.S. Census report, 13.6 million Americans are single parents. Raising your child alone is a time-consuming and exhaustive process. Single parents must set clear priorities, be well organized, and be pros at time management. They also have to find the right balance between work, home, children, and free time.

Tip: Take a much needed break every day. Get enough sleep, exercise daily, and eat healthy foods. Give yourself enough time to regroup and de-stress.

Support System Strategies

Be the Boss—Don't let your child run the show; your child is not your peer.

Reign In—Stability and predictability.

Contacts—Build a reliable network of family, friends, and co-workers.

To do or not to do—Make lists, daily agendas, and keep to an established schedule.

Engagements—Communicate openly with your children. Let them know you need their help with chores and arranging mutually agreeable times for activities.

Escapes—Cooperative parenting encourages guiltless free time.

Divorce Decorum

What is the topic of divorce doing in a book about mastering good manners? Plenty! Your marriage may be irretrievably broken, but your parental relationship is forever. It is well documented that the way you and your former spouse interact with each other is crucial to your child's post-divorce adjustment. Children from a divorced home have the same needs as children from an intact home. All children need respect, affection, clear boundaries, and discipline. Put your child's feelings up front—communicate effectively by giving open and honest feedback.

For your child's sake, demonstrating mutual respect with your former partner will enable your child to grow up emotionally healthy. Remember, your negative feelings toward your former partner are *not your child's problem*. This is the time you must learn to act; your child doesn't need to be a part of the drama.

Civility is the glue that connects children's strength and security.

There are no ex-parents, just ex-spouses.
—Doc Jodi

Divorce Civility Do's

Always—Focus on what's best for your child.
Always—Encourage your child to spend time with the other parent.
Always—Help your child remember the other parent's birthday and Mother's/Father's Day.
Always—Reach out to the child's other set of grandparents and relatives.
Always—Be on time for pick—ups and drop-offs.
Always—Reassure your child that he/she is not at fault for the divorce.

Divorce Civility Don'ts

Never—Put your child in the middle.
Never—Pass checks, money, or notes through your child.
Never—Ask your child to snoop for you.
Never—Communicate anger and hostility about your former partner in front of your child.
Never—Criticize your former partner's family members in front of your child.
Never—Overindulge your child with gifts or money out of guilt.

Tip: During and following a period of divorce, regaining control of your household is paramount. Keep schedules as usual and stick to old routines.

Work together to establish a "business relationship" with your former partner. It will take the emotions out of the interactions. Do not ask children to choose sides and do not allow them to pit one parent against the other. The residual damage has a lifetime effect.
—Coach Lori

Tip: Take a blank calendar and color code the days your child will be with each parent, including vacations and holidays. The key is to let your child pick the colors and make it personal. Hang the calendar up so the child knows where he will be each day.

The secret of raising an emotionally healthy child of divorce is dependent on the speed of "normalcy" brought into her routine, limited arguing between parents, and an acknowledgment by the parents that children suffer, too!
—Doc Jodi

If you and your spouse are unable to develop a parenting plan, a professional can help you. A parenting plan mediates the time and place of visitations, social/medical/educational needs, and how parents are to communicate.

The correct way to introduce a former spouse is:

"Carly, this is my former husband, Luke."
"Ali, this is Dylan's mother, Claudia."

CHAPTER NINE

IT'S A FAMILY AFFAIR

Blending Families—How to Cater to Everyone

Blended families are the merging of a new family, combining all respective children. Most couples are unaware of critical issues involved in the blending process. Problems arise with the merging of different values, ideals, and customs.

The idea of the Brady Bunch family (living happily ever after) or Cinderella (Wicked Stepmother Syndrome) are extremes and not the norm.

Cool Approach:
OBSERVE: Learn the new family dynamics to interact appropriately.
UNIFY: Present as united and stable.
SHARE: Respect space and privacy.
RESOLVE: Beware of loyalty conflicts.
ENVISION: Discuss the future of the family.
DIVERSIFY: Spend alone time with each child.
EVOLVE: Establish new family customs and snapshots.
ACCEPT: Make sure your child maintains a healthy relationship with the non-residential parent.
CREATE: Similar rules that work for both families.

Un-Cool Approach:
PRESSURE: Avoid pushing the new relationship on the child.
FORCE: Never insist your children call the new parent Mom or Dad.
ARGUE: Stay neutral and don't show parental conflict in front of the child.
IGNORE: Don't forget to cultivate your marital relationship.
RESIST: Disciplining your stepchild when possible; that responsibility should belong to the biological parent.
AVOID: Keeping secrets from other family members.

FACTS OF THE MANNER:

64% of all families are blended families. In fact, 1/3 of all children nationwide will become part of a blended family before graduating high school.

Children under 10 have an easier transition and are more accepting of a new adult in the family.

Adolescents ages 10 to 14 have the most difficult time adjusting.

Older teens who are separating from "parent" needs to "peer" needs have an easier time adjusting to new parent households.

Boys tend to accept new families more readily than girls.

Females tend to feel uncomfortable receiving affection from a stepfather.

Boys and girls sometimes prefer verbal praise rather than physical closeness.

Closing the Generation Gap

The Step-Grandparent Gap Trap: Pointers for Parents' Parents

Grandparents in a blended family have an active role in supporting the new parental relationship. It is imperative for grandparents to follow the new family rules and not bring up the past, especially in front of the new spouse and children. This is hurtful and will typically build barriers that are difficult to overcome. It takes time to build love and respect for all family members concerned. Step-grandparents can be a wonderful resource in a new blended family.

Participating in these phases will help make your transition even smoother:

The **"Who Are You?" Phase:** Spend special alone time with new grandchildren to learn about their likes and dislikes, friends, etc.
The **"What's Going On?" Phase:** Be flexible and sensitive to changes in routine and children's behavior.
The **"Stake Out Your Territory" Phase:** Don't compete with biological grandparents; follow the parents lead—they're running the show now.
The **"Who's In Charge?" Phase:** Be ready to bite your tongue and follow the rules parents make. Learn the family's rules, support them, and stick to them.
The **"Play No Favorites" Phase:** Strive to treat ALL grandchildren equally.

When families do not live close by, using a webcam and Skype technology can keep you connected. This also enables your family to share special occasions and holidays together.

—Doc Jodi

CHAPTER TEN

ACHIEVEMENT OVERDRIVE

Finding the Right Balance

If you feel you are trapped in the insanity of "achievement overdrive," you are not alone. Some parents feel their children need to be doing productive things **all the time**. So many lessons—tennis, ballet, and karate, oh my, music, dance, basketball. Is your child really gaining an advantage in life, or is he headed for a breakdown by the age of ten? Some parents even have spreadsheets on the refrigerator to remind them where each child is headed after school! How much is TOO much?

Young children are not emotionally equipped to deal with such highly structured and demanding schedules. This is the time when they are learning how to cope with everyday life skills. Think about it: how many adults do you know with excessive structure and demanding schedules who aren't emotional wrecks?

Most experts agree that there is intense pressure for children to over-achieve. What seems to matter most to many parents is how quickly their child's "Resume of Accomplishments" is growing. They sacrifice quality for quantity of achievements. Even worse, they become blinded to the difference between satisfying and terrifying to the child by pushing them too hard, too fast. Finding the *right balance* for you and your family is essential.

Steer your family away from Achievement Overdrive and stay connected with:

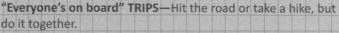

"We're all in this together" DINNERS—Serve these up at least once a week.
Parent–Child SPECIAL TIME—It doesn't get more personal than 1:1 alone time.
Fun time GAME NIGHTS—Families that play together, stay together.
Feel-good WORKOUTS—Sweat things out together.
"Everyone's on board" TRIPS—Hit the road or take a hike, but do it together.
Choose your CAUSE DAYS—Volunteer together at community events.
Create your own CELEBRATIONS—Come up with new family traditions to honor.
"What's on your mind?" MEETINGS—Keep those lines of communication open.

Parents, please! Let your children BE children. There's plenty of time down the road for your 5-year-old to take classes in Mandarin Chinese and scholarship preparation. After-school sports and other activities offer an excellent alternative to expensive, private lessons. Additionally, they help create new school friendships for your child.

—Coach Lori

Parents often say that children complain of boredom. As an anecdote to their boredom, encourage independent activities at home such as gardening, model building, and jigsaw puzzles. Boredom is a state of mind.

—Doc Jodi

Family Meetings Matter

Family meetings take planning and cooperation from all family members and all members must attend:

- ✓ They are held weekly at the same time and place.
- ✓ Each person takes a turn running a meeting.
- ✓ No distractions like cell phones, TV, games, etc.
- ✓ End the family meeting with a fun activity or dessert.
- ✓ Find a way to allow each person to speak without being interrupted.
- ✓ Usual topics are: New News, Old News, Commendations, and any special topics, like finances and family outings or vacation announcements/suggestions.

Check it out:

Diego's Family Meeting
Leader __Dad__ Date __3/12__

Old Business- The computer was not fixed - why?

New Business- Mom sprained her ankle which means she will need a hand around the house.

Weekly Goal- Midterm week, Limit chores, Easy meals, Quiet house, Tutors

Commendations- Victor has been keeping his room clean. Luke has been on time everyday.

Chapter Eleven

RULING THE ROOST

Don't be Chicken to Teach Good Manners

Teaching your child good manners is your job. But do you really understand the true meaning of good manners ... and how they will inevitably influence your child's life? Manners are actions and words that show people you care about them. Good manners are not just for the sake of *looking good* but rather how they will impact your child's future with others—emotionally, socially and professionally.

When children learn the importance of good manners and are able to master them effectively, a legacy is passed down from generation to generation. This legacy perpetuates **respect** within the family, home, self, community, and the world. For this to work, good manners have to be an "important value" to **you** as parents.

Everyday Courtesies are Becoming Uncommon

Our society will continue to deteriorate if manners and common courtesies aren't made a priority. Common courtesies, frequently spoken without purpose, ultimately lose their meaning. The reactions people have when they hear and appreciate the sincere expression of courtesy become the **magic behind the words.** Good manners are contagious—you have to give it to receive it. **Say it and mean it!**

Magic Words:

- ✓ Please
- ✓ Thank you
- ✓ Excuse me
- ✓ You're welcome

- ✓ I'm sorry
- ✓ It's nice to meet you
- ✓ How are you?
- ✓ How was your day?

When everyone in the household puts the magic words to work and uses them daily, it creates contagious manner moments that foster mutual respect in the home.

—Coach Lori

Putting Magic Words to Work

Magic Words of Encouragement—"I am so proud of you"; "You put in such good effort,"; "Doesn't that make you feel good?"

Magic Words that Show Children Respect for Adults—"Thank you, Mr. Smith, for letting us use your basketball hoop"; "Mrs. O'Brian, you're so cool for taking us to the movies."

Magic Words of Empathy—"I'm sorry I hurt your feelings"; "Mommy is sorry she disappointed you."

Children are great imitators—they embellish the words they hear to get their parents' attention. Therefore, parents must stop and think before using foul language in front of children. Show zero tolerance for curse words. Explain in a firm voice that these words are unacceptable.

Why Aren't Your Kids Pitching In?

 Because you don't hold them accountable! Keeping the *common areas* neat cannot be negotiated. Delegating chores to children contributes to a home environment that validates the importance of each individual family member and encourages a sense of accountability. Working together teaches teamwork and responsibility, invaluable life skills needed later in life. Chores aren't always fun, and should never be considered a punishment.

Allowing your child to speed clean his or her room in 10 seconds flat, and letting that pass for acceptable, does not teach time management. Make house rules clear and state precisely what is expected of each member. Post chores where they are visible, stating each chore, the family member responsible, and completion time. Break down chores into simple steps for young children.

Consistency is key. There are no negotiations regarding chores. Parents work and children need to pitch in to do their fair share to keep the house clean. Besides, it teaches commitment and respect for the other household members.

—Coach Lori

Chart Your Chore Course of Action

Make chores feel rewarding: Follow through and acknowledge chore completion with rewards such as Good Manners stickers.

Spin the "Wheel of Chores": Make a rotation wheel—where it lands is the chore they've earned.

Create Chore Curiosity: Use child-size equipment to get children interested.

Play Job Jar Jeopardy: Take the pressure off yourself by allowing children to control their own fate. Let them choose chores no one else wants by picking them randomly from a jar filled with tasks you want to have done.

Taking responsibility should start as young as 2 years old:

Ages 2–5

LAUNDRY DEPOSITS—Teaching children to put dirty clothes into the laundry basket will help their development rather than hamper it.

MAKING THE BED—So many people are falling asleep on the job these days. Maybe it's because their parents didn't let them make their own bed.

SETTING THE TABLE—Children can put out napkins and silverware. The message is you can't eat without utensils.

TRASH IT—Having your child throw away snack wrappers and cups is always a great idea to toss out.

RECYCLE—It's important for humankind and the environment, so make sure your kids have "bin there and done that."

Ages 5–8

TAKE A LOAD OFF—Asking your child to unload the dishwasher or clothes dryer can help take the pressure off of you.

LAUNDRY DELIVERY—Your child is old enough to put his or her own clothes away.

REMOTE LOCATIONS—Remote controls and portable phones should find their way back to where they originally started.

TABLE CLEARING—It's a simple concept: you cook, they clear.

FOUL TOWELS—Wet towels don't belong on the floor.

PET SMART—Get everyone involved to feed and walk the family pet.

Ages 9 & Up

ALL OF THE ABOVE ... and don't let them off the hook!

DECO-STORAGE—Decorate clothes hampers with your child. Recycle and decorate large containers for toys.

Flushing Out Bad Manners

Cleaning bathrooms is a dirty job, but someone has to do it. Meaning: Everyone has to do it. Wiping down the sink and counters may be boring, but eventually it does become an automatic task. Flushing the toilet and putting the seat down is not only good manners, it is also essential hygiene. Even simple things like putting the cap back on the toothpaste tube and wiping the hand soap that dripped all over the counter add up to making a big difference in developing bathroom pride. Remember, some people say you can judge a restaurant by how clean the restroom is. What kind of impression does your bathroom make on guests?

Private bathroom manners

- ✓ Always knock on the door before entering.
- ✓ Don't hog the bathroom.
- ✓ Clean the toilet seat.
- ✓ Teach boys to put the seat down when finished.

Public restroom manners

- ✓ Never let your child go to the bathroom himself.
- ✓ Clean up after yourself.
- ✓ Always flush the toilet.
- ✓ Never flush sanitary napkins or tampons down the toilet.
- ✓ Don't talk about others—you never know who's in the next stall.
- ✓ Always wash hands before leaving the restroom.
- ✓ Always throw dirty diapers in the proper receptacles.

A Peek into Privacy

Respecting others' privacy is the basic tenet of **trust**. Privacy is earned by levels of responsibility and trustworthiness. While this is culturally variable, parents must set privacy parameters for sleeping arrangements, closed doors, knocking, and personal situations. Parents need private time and children must be taught to knock, and wait, for a response before entering their room. Knocking on closed doors shows *mutual respect.* Parents must always secure adult material and keep adult conversation under wraps.

When children begin to close their own bedroom and bathroom door, in most cases, this is a signal that *they want* privacy. Modesty should be encouraged as children develop. Children will let you know when they feel uncomfortable with nudity. Take that hint—cover yourself and allow them to bathe and change in private.

Snooping should never be done by parents unless there is a cause for concern for safety or security. On the other hand, parents should know who their children's friends are, where they live, and something about their family. **This is an important rule to establish before they go off unsupervised with their friends.**

Another word about privacy. As children mature, they have the need to be alone with friends behind closed doors. They seek privacy as a way to feel more independent.

Avoid going through their personal belongings, journals, text messages, and emails. However, if you are suspicious that your child is engaging in the use of drugs, alcohol, gambling, pornography, sexting, stealing, or having inappropriate contact online, it is your parental obligation to intervene.

Private Possessions

What can be more frustrating than the sounds of children fighting over possessions taken without asking? Teach children to respect others' possessions and insist that they ask before borrowing. There can be no exception to this rule! Also, you cannot negate this rule by asking one child to retrieve something from another sibling's space. It is still an invasion of privacy.

If children lose, break, or ruin another's borrowed possession, it's their responsibility to replace it. Parents should not replace it as it will not teach the child the value of taking care of a borrowed possession. This possession can be replaced by money in the piggy bank or by earning it through extra chores.

—*Coach Lori*

Tip: It is important that every family member ask before borrowing anything from another family member; even something as simple as lipstick or earbuds.

CHAPTER TWELVE

IMPRESS EXPRESS

You have only 15 seconds to make a great first impression. That's it—and WHAM!—the other party has you all sized up. How many times have you struggled to make eye contact or failed to get someone's full attention because the other person is paying attention to something else, fidgeting with their pocket change, yawning away, or fiddling with their cell phone? Be honest, are you guilty of any of those things, too?

Teaching children how to acknowledge others with respect is an important life skill and a fundamental precursor for success. Using "please," "thank you," and "excuse me," and not interrupting when someone else is speaking, will make a positive lasting impression. And the most important message this demonstrates to your child is "How am I making the other person feel?" Before a person can **EARN** respect, he or she must first learn how to **GIVE** respect.

Respect begins by teaching children the importance of:

NAMES—Children should call their parents Mom and Dad.
TITLES—Address adults by using their title: Mr., Mrs., Ms., Dr., Reverend, Rabbi, etc.
AGES—Introduce the eldest person to the youngest person.
SINCERITY—Use eye contact/facial expressions to show genuine interest.

Handshake Your Way to a Great Impression

Teach your child to extend his right hand when meeting an adult unless instructed otherwise. A firm handshake (for men and women) reaffirms a positive sense of self.

Know the difference between a personal (casual) and a 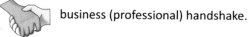 business (professional) handshake.

Teach and practice the art of making a great first impression. Smile; let the other person know you are glad to see them, and say "Hello" warmly with eye contact. Make sure to rehearse saying the other person's name at least once during the conversation.

Give your child's teacher a reason to be impressed with her at first meeting. Both of you should greet the teacher on the first day, have all your child's supplies on hand, and be dressed appropriately.

Tip: Don't fumble! If you forget someone's name during introductions, simply introduce those you do know and wait for the others to introduce themselves.

First impressions are vital in all professional meetings. At a college or first job interview, business professionals expect a firm handshake, which shows confidence and maturity. Remember that corporate America still hires poised, self-assured, and courteous candidates. Imagine how confident your child's handshake will be if he starts practicing now.

—Coach Lori

Time Considerations

If you cannot be on time—be early! Organization is the secret. Knowing where you need to be, and what you've got to do to get there on time, is critical to preventing your schedule from spiraling out of control.

It is extremely rude and discourteous to run late. Everyone has an emergency from time to time that can make them late, but no one should run late all the time. Everyone's time is valuable, so when you are running late, please be responsible and phone the person(s) waiting for you.

Plan your exit—Getting out the door on time requires single tasking, not multitasking.

Expect the unexpected—Anticipate that things happen, and leave plenty of time.

Eat on time—Be on time for restaurant reservations—you're holding everyone else up.

Manage your own time better—Children learn time management from their parents.

First things first—Allow children to watch TV or play games after they are all ready to walk out the door.

Tip: Don't waste your time looking for cell phones, keys, etc. Put your on-the-go items on a hook or basket by the door.

CHAPTER THIRTEEN

ETIQUETTE NEVER GETS OLD

What Ever Happened to Respecting Your Elders?

Believe it or not, there is an astonishing amount of prejudice against the elderly in our society. And without proper intervention it will keep on growing. There is a big difference between *informal* and *inconsiderate* behavior regarding elders. With parents and grandparents living longer, new economic, health, and social issues will potentially impact your family.

> **Be someone's guest**—Create situations where you and your children visit older adults.
> **Extend common courtesies**—Hold doors open and allow older adults to sit first.
> **Give it up**—If an elderly person is standing, give them your seat.
> **Cook with caution**—Be sensitive to the dietary needs of elder adults because they could become ill.

Grand Parenting

Today, one-third of all adults are grandparents and they can be as young as forty-five years old. This connection links family history and tradition, and the grandparent relationship is the second most important relationship a child has. Whether grandparents live near or far away, keep your children in touch with them. Not all parents have a good relationship with their parents. You don't have to like your child's grandparents, but you do have to be respectful and allow *them* to enjoy the relationship. Many children feel close to their grandparents and confide in them.

For healthy grandparent relationships the following needs to occur:

Honor yearly—Honor National Grandparents Day; make a fuss.
Call often—Call grandparents weekly because they may feel alone and lonely.
Invite often—Involve grandparents in your child's school activities.
Involve often—Make older relatives feel welcome during family celebrations.
Enjoy endlessly—Encourage extended periods of time with your child and their grandparents.

If you are mending a broken relationship with your parents and/or grandparents, *please heed this read*:

✓ Do not argue with your parents in front of your children.
✓ Do not use your child as a pawn. Grandparents should see their grandchildren.
✓ Do not put your child in the middle of a strained relationship.

Pass on special family grandparent moments:

✓ Provide grandparents with 4x6 index cards and ask them to fill out "Wisdom Cards." These cards are a collection of special memories to be passed on through generations.
✓ Collect grandparents' favorite recipes and ask for the history of the recipe.
✓ Ask grandparents and your children to help put together a Family Tree.
✓ Encourage special alone time with each grandparent.

Do Your In-laws Drive You Insane?

Did you realize that when you said, "I do," you were marrying more than one person? You don't have to get a divorce because of your in-laws! Simply stated, your loyalty should shift appropriately— your spouse comes first. In most marriages there will be input, solicited or not, by both sides of the family. In most families, there will always be jealousy, competition, hurt feelings, and even injustice. No one gets along with everyone all the time.

State clear parameters with your spouse regarding household rules, especially guidelines for your children. Personal issues between you and your spouse should <u>not</u> be disclosed to in-laws. As with any new relationship it takes time to build feelings of mutual respect. Convey a positive attitude and enlist your spouse for ideas in engaging his/her family.

Demonstrate mutual respect by setting personal boundaries

No sugar—coating—Let your partner know how you feel.
Wrap it up!—Use cues between you and your partner to end a visit.
Know when to bite your tongue—Don't criticize your in-laws in front of your children.
Keep the peace—Be sensitive to your partner's familial relationships, and encourage your partner to visit alone.
Mayday! Mayday!—If an in-law is toxic to your well-being, distance yourself.
Balancing loyalties—Take turns for holidays, trips, and special occasions.
And if all else fails—Be the bigger person and suck it up!

68

Domestic and Support Personnel

Did you hear about the heiress who was charged with abusing her housekeeper? Not once, but twice. Not only in front of her children, but in front of her housekeeper's children! And then there was a top fashion model who threw a cell phone at her housekeeper.

Many households depend on nannies or domestic help, and this support team must be respected. Plus, having help in the home does not preclude children from doing chores. Even the children in the White House are expected to make their own beds.

Remember to extend courtesy to all the people who provide services at your home including doormen, newspaper/mail carriers, delivery drivers, gardeners, etc. The way *you* treat the people who work for you is the way your *child* will treat them. Always acknowledge others with a smile or nod, and greet respectfully. Ask personnel how they would like to be addressed and respect it. If possible, remember a birthday, holiday, or special event regarding the people who help you.

Chapter Fourteen

MI CASA, SU CASA

Okay, your overnight guests are about to arrive. Now what? Are you a gracious host? The key is taking the guess work out of guest work. Make guests feel like *your* home is *their* home.

Figure out what you and your children need to do to roll out the "Welcome Mat" so everyone feels comfortable. Make sure to cover:

Sleeping over—Where they will be sleeping and where will their belongings go?

It's their room—Respect their privacy.

Finding it—Familiarize guests with where phones, TV computer, food, and other necessities and conveniences can be found.

It's their children—Your guests must discipline their own children.

Clear rules—Inform your guests of the rules everyone in your home follows.

And what if you are the guest?

Don't arrive empty—handed—Bring something! Flowers or cookies always generate a smile.

Be punctual—Arrive and leave on time.

Learn to obey—Explain the host family's house rules to your children.

Pitch in—Always ask how you can help.

Bathroom musts—Don't snoop around and don't use their personal shower products. Rinse out the tub and sink after use.

Come Prepared—Bring a special thank-you note or card to fill out when you leave your host's home.

Don't Fall Asleep on the Job

Sleepovers are a right of passage for every child. Certain house rules must be made clear to your child and then reiterated with your child and guest. Reinforce basic courtesies such as keeping common areas neat. Very young children need more structured activities.

Not everyone likes to follow rules, so keep them short and clear, and present them as pleasantly as possible.

- ✓ No jumping on the bed.
- ✓ No playing ball in the house.
- ✓ Specify off-limit areas.
- ✓ Ask permission before using the computer, raiding the refrigerator, or helping yourself to snacks.
- ✓ Explain pet rules.
- ✓ Set clear guidelines for sibling involvement.

Security Blanket to Go

Your child may be asked to be a house guest as early as 5 years of age. He or she should be comfortable and familiar with the host's family. Prepare your child in advance for a positive experience. Explain that rules vary from home to home, depending on the parents.

Some children will jump at the chance of sleeping out, while others are hesitant to go. Talk it over with your child. If your child needs to bring his favorite stuffed animal, let him. Allow your child to call home, and never tease your child about his level of discomfort or insecurity.

—Doc Jodi

Sleepover success at a friend's home depends on whether you:

> **Stick to the invited guest list**—Don't bring uninvited guests.
> **Tick-tock, watch the clock**—Arrive and leave on time.
> **No pigging out**—Remind your child not to hog the food. You don't want his friend's parents to think you don't feed him.
> **Keep curiosity in check**—Teach your child that spying on her friend's sibling or snooping through drawers is a no-no.
> **Cage the stoolpigeon**—Make sure all kids know that tattling and teasing will not be tolerated.

Remember to ask:

> What other adults will be present in the home?
> Who will babysit the children if the parents are not home?
> Are there weapons in the home?
> What guidelines do you have for what is and isn't allowed during a sleepover?
> What time should I pick my child up? (And BE THERE!)

Tip: You know you've done a great job when the host parent calls to say, "Your child has the best manners and when can she come again?"

Remember to tell:

> Emergency contact information
> Allergies and sensitivity precautions
> Fears, phobias, or panic triggers

Birthday Bashes and Party Bloopers

Emotions run high for everyone on special occasions, especially birthdays. The younger the child the more difficult it is to control these emotions. Be sensitive to your child's excitement and form realistic expectations. For children under 5 years old, these expectations should be kept at a minimum. The number of children to be invited should correspond to age. However, when inviting classmates make certain to invite ALL the children.

Birthday parties must not be competitive or extravagant. Five-year-olds should not be picked up in a limo and taken to a day spa for a makeover.

Party Perfect

AGE CONSIDERATIONS—Make birthday parties age appropriate.
A DREAM THEME—Plan the theme according to age/ability.
BE CLEAR—Specify the name(s) of invited guest(s). Specify whether an adult should be in attendance or a sibling is included.

GREAT EXPECTATIONS—Your child's party wishes should be discussed with your child continuously from invitations to date of event.

PARTY PLANNER—Pre-plan the schedule of the party event.

ACTIVITY GOALS—Organize activities that leave NO CHILD OUT.

SUPERVISING RESPONSIBILITIES—Have other responsible adults there to help you keep order.

GREAT STARTS—Greet each guest personally.

GIFT WRAP—When opening gifts, teach your child to show appreciation.

GRACIOUS GOOD—BYES—As the party host, it is your duty to thank each person for coming.

Guest Perfect

DO THE RIGHT THING—You must RSVP when it is required.

SMART CHOICE—Let your child help pick out the birthday gift.

GET IT RIGHT—Before the party, go over all birthday party rules.

TIME IT RIGHT—Arrive on time and say "Happy Birthday" to the birthday child.

MORE OF THE RIGHT THING—Ask host parents if guest parents are expected to stay and leave uninvited siblings at home.

ATTITUDE ADJUSTMENT—Remind your child that it is someone else's birthday; therefore, their gifts are not his gifts.

GIVE IT RIGHT—Have your child present the gift to the birthday girl or boy.

MINGLE ROOM—Ease your child into the group setting.

Example:

Sophie showed up at the bowling alley for a birthday party with her son and his two younger brothers. Not only were the younger siblings disruptive but, as uninvited guests, were a burden to the party host.

Example:
John was invited to Sam's party and had responded he would attend. Another invitation came for the same date and time. Most of John's friends were going to the second party. John's parents insisted he go to the initial invite to honor the prior commitment.

Tip: Parents should always instill the importance of honoring a prior commitment once made.

When your child is not invited to a party, it is imperative to validate his feelings of disappointment. Although it is very hurtful to your child, you should not take it personally. Use this opportunity to explain that not all children are invited to all parties.

—*Doc Jodi*

The Writing Ritual

Thank-You Notes

Why Write?

Taking the time to write shows good breeding. It acknowledges appreciation and expresses gratitude to the gift giver for their effort and expense of the gift.

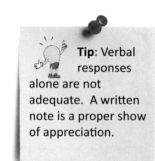

Tip: Verbal responses alone are not adequate. A written note is a proper show of appreciation.

When to Write

The most appropriate time is as soon as you receive the gift. If you wait you may forget. Plus, the longer you put it off, the less important it will feel, and the less enthusiastic you will be when you finally do get around to writing.

How to Write

Proper protocol is to use black or blue ink and the note should come from your child in his or her own handwriting. However, if your child is very young, using a crayon is acceptable.

Examples of creative thank-you notes:
Fill in a blank thank-you note post card.
Children's own artwork is especially appreciated.
Include a photo, preferably taken at the party.
Assist your child to create personalized stationary.

What to Write

1. Address the card with the person's name/title.
2. Thank the person for the gift (be specific).
3. When thanking someone for a monetary gift, do not mention the amount given—just for the generous gift.
4. State why the gift meant so much to you.
5. Sign the card personally.

Tip: A family calendar not only lists family activities, but should include friends and family birthdays, anniversaries, and other special occasions. Make sending out cards together a family ritual.

Tip: Email is not always personal enough. If you must email, send something creative from an online card service where you can design something using your own words.

Your older child will eventually fill out a job application, apply for a summer job, or apply for college admission. After a college or job interview, a thank you letter must be written within 24 hours thanking the interviewer for their time spent and reiterating interest in the position or admission.

Word of caution; be particularly careful of correct spelling (especially names and titles) and mailing the letter in the correct envelope with the matching addressee.

There is nothing more impressive to an interviewer than receiving a thank-you letter after an interview.

—Coach Lori

Chapter Fifteen

TECHTRONIC TROUBLES

Calling Up the Right Manners

Establish a new direction for high-tech interference. In order to foster better quality family time, you just have to put all other conversations and messages on hold.

Don't accept phone calls:
- ✓ During mealtime
- ✓ After a designated hour
- ✓ During family meetings or events

Teaching children how to properly answer the phone is an important life skill.

Mommy's in the bathroom!!!

Phone manner steps:
- ✓ Let your child know that there is a real person on the other end of the phone even though she is not seen.
- ✓ Using a toy phone, role play with your child and teach him how to speak slowly and clearly.
- ✓ Supervise your child until he has mastered this critical phone concept.

Teach children:
- ✓ Strangers and solicitors should be told a polite "no thank you," followed by a dial tone.
- ✓ Never give out personal or household information.
- ✓ Never say you're alone at home.
- ✓ Emergency drill 911... Know it!

During family meetings or events

When your child is ready to be a "family receptionist," practice proper phone etiquette by role playing with a toy phone.

Practice the following script with your child:

> **Phone Tone**
>
> "Hi, this is Malia, who is this, please?"
>
> "Just a moment, please."
>
> "She/He can't come to the phone right now."
>
> "Can you please call back later?"

Analyzing Your Child's "Calling Plan"

The Symptoms

Your children will not use cell phones responsibly if you don't! The 2006 ABC News, *20/20* survey, "Rudeness in America" (available online), suggests that speaking loudly on cell phones is the number one irritating behavior. And a recent Sprint survey revealed: 80% of wireless callers have become less courteous. However, 97% do not feel they are the offender.

Are you part of the 97% who offend others by ranting, raving, and rambling on your cell phone?

Okay, time to look in the mirror again. How many of the following are you guilty of?

YAPPING on your cell phone at the gym while exercising.

ARGUING with your significant other or friends while shopping or running errands.

BLABBING (or texting) during movie previews or while watching TV with others.

RINGING in public everywhere from restaurants to funerals where your phone should be off or at least on vibrate.

DISTRACTING yourself (and others) from what you're supposed to be doing.

The "Side Effects" Can Be Hazardous to Your Health

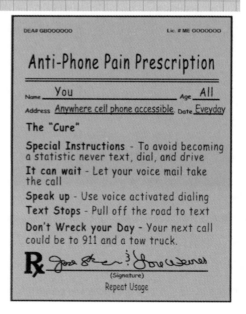

DEA# GB000000   Lic. # ME 0000000

Anti-Phone Pain Prescription

Name ___You___   Age ___All___
Address _Anywhere cell phone accessible._ Date _Eveyday_

The "Cure"

Special Instructions - To avoid becoming a statistic never text, dial, and drive
It can wait - Let your voice mail take the call
Speak up - Use voice activated dialing
Text Stops - Pull off the road to text
Don't Wreck your Day - Your next call could be to 911 and a tow truck.

R̶x̶ _____
(Signature)
Repeat Usage

The remedy for cell phone rudeness:

> **Change your tone**—Eliminate obnoxious rings.
>
> **Lights out, phones off**—That means movies, concerts, theater shows, and other public gatherings.
>
> **Stop noise pollution**—No one wants to hear your conversations, especially at a high volume.
>
> **Take a rest**—Keep cell phones off during meals.

What to Cell Your Kids On ...

Many times, cell phones provide peace of mind for parents. Wireless companies offer special kiddies' cell phones for children as young as five for safety and emergencies that are also loaded with parental controls. Whatever the age, your child's cell phone must be managed, monitored, and respected.

Manage:

> ✓ Open the account in your name, not your child's name.
> ✓ Turn off the camera feature.
> ✓ Give to child only for safety, emergencies, and to update you regarding their whereabouts.

Monitor:

> ✓ Let children know you are tracking their calls.
> ✓ Check regularly for sexually explicit photos, unsuitable texting/sexting dialogue, and adult content.
> ✓ Instruct your child to answer the phone every time you call.
> ✓ Have your child ask for permission before texting and downloading games.

Make Limits:

- ✓ Prohibit use of cell phones in class.
- ✓ Discuss child bullying with your child. Make sure he knows to report any threats to you. Make it clear that if he uses the phone to threaten or bully another child, he and his cell phone will be grounded.
- ✓ Know and abide by your school district's rules on cell phone usage. Be aware that students are in class texting, cheating and worse.

Replacing your child's cell phone whenever it breaks does not teach responsibility or accountability. "You break it or lose it, you pay for it."
—Doc Jodi

Managing Phone Messages

The messages that come from your phone are perceived as a direct reflection on you. Are you leaving the impression you really want to leave when your voicemail answers? Does your child's messages send the right message … or do they leave something to be desired?

Outgoing Messages: Don't have lengthy messages, jokes, or singing toddlers.

Leaving Messages: Be careful of the message you leave, others WILL hear it.

Returning Calls: Be prompt getting back to callers. Someone called you for a reason, even if it was just to say "Hello." It is rude to get back to them days later. When you do call someone, think about what you're going to say if you get their machine. Listening to someone rambling on or just breathing while they're trying to find the right words is borrrrrring!

Wanted: Parents Who Talk—Not Text

According to a recent Nielsen Mobile survey, for the first time ever, people are texting more than they are talking. In fact, the average teen texts a staggering 2,200 times per month!

Texting Do's:

- ✓ Confirm a play date.
- ✓ Have accessibility to your child.
- ✓ Limit monthly text messages.
- ✓ Know that texts are traceable like emails.

Texting Don'ts:

- ✓ Answer texts from strangers.
- ✓ Ever use **text** to avoid a difficult situation.
- ✓ Repeatedly text in front of your children.
- ✓ Texting while driving—EVER.
- ✓ Allow texting to replace face-to-face socialization.
- ✓ Text at the dinner table.

Repeatedly texting others in front of your children sends the message, "You are not important to talk to," or "We don't have anything to talk about." When people rely solely on texting to communicate, the mastery of face-to-face socialization becomes lost.

Are you aware that 67% of teens admitted to texting while driving at high speeds? Recently, a commuter train crashed killing and injuring hundreds of people while the conductor was texting through a stop sign. Do you remember when MADD (Mothers Against Drunk Driving) was formed after a mother's child was killed by a drunk driver? Today, there needs to be a new organization—MATD (Mothers Against Texting Drivers). This alarming trend of texting while driving is rampant among teen drivers. If your child witnesses YOU doing this, he will think this is permissible behavior. Well, it's not—it's deadly behavior! *Unconsciously, parents set a dangerous and unlawful precedent for mobile mismanagement.*

Breaking the Text Code

It's 9:00 P.M. Do you know who your children are texting, what pictures they are sending, and what they are saying? It is a mistake for parents to think that their child is safe in his own bedroom. This can be a minefield for parents to maneuver, but if you don't, the results for your family could be explosive.

Sexting Scares

According to Wikipedia, "Sexting is the act of sending sexually explicit messages or photos electronically, typically between cell phones." Children as young as eleven are engaging in this disturbing trend without understanding its consequences. This reckless behavior is ruining children's reputations, while the photos are landing in the hands of adult sexual predators. When a child is caught downloading or forwarding these photos, they can be arrested, tried, and convicted as a sex offender. Furthermore, once in cyberspace, these explicit

photos become permanently etched in your child's file for all to see—
a college admission's officer or future employer.

The new lingo for texting, instant messaging, and blogging is difficult to learn even for the savviest mom and dad. Parents should keep up with the new language kids use to communicate with each other.

ALERT

Sexual Acronyms:
LH6—Let's have sex
P911—Parents coming into room—alert
CD9 or PAW—Parents around, Parents are watching
POS—Parents over shoulder
420—Let's get high; Marijuana
8—Oral sex
IGHT—I got high tonight
NIFOC—Naked in front of the computer
TDTM—Talk dirty to me
GNOC—Get naked on Cam (Webcam)

Drug Slang:
A—LSD
A/boot—Under the influence of drugs
AC/DC—Codeine cough syrup
ACE or African—Marijuana cigarette
Adam—Meth
Agonies—Withdrawal
Al Capone—Heroin
Angel (all derivatives)—PCP (clear hallucinogen)

Tip: Keep up with the lingo:

Web sites:
www.netlingo.com;
www.NoSlang.com

Software:
TeenChatDecoder5.0

Netiquette

Staying Safe in Cyberspace

 Limited knowledge of Cyberspace safety puts parents and children at risk. Children today encounter sexual predators and cyber-bullies lurking behind their computer screens. Bullies used to only be a physical threat at school on the playground and in neighborhoods, but now, are also alive and well on the Internet. Many children and teens have experienced breakdowns, problems with the law and suicide attempts, all associated with Internet use.

Many parents are not aware of Internet evils. Children often have unlimited, and certainly unsupervised, computer time. Parents are pressured by their children to give them Internet access. They will hide in their rooms and sit for hours "chatting" with friends and strangers. They wander into unsupervised chat rooms and popular social networking sites.

Popular social networking sites have become the "new mall hangout." All postings and photos immediately become public domain and part of your very public online history. Future college admissions and employment recruiters can access this information. Parents need to be aware of all social networking sites, some of which are: Club Penguin, Facebook, MySpace, YouTube, and all blogging sites.

Be Your Child's Watchdog on the Web:

Learn all you can and stay on top of the latest trends, social hangouts, scams, and dangers to children.

Connect with your child:

Explain real relationships vs. virtual relationships—Make sure your child understands the differences between real-world friendships compared to anonymous virtual friendships.

Give surfing lessons—Teach children that "surfers" can be strangers.

Draw up a computer contract—Discuss limits and boundaries in an oral or written agreement.

Perform regular check-ups—Let children know you have access to their computer.

Do your download diligence—Tell children they need your permission to download software.

Maintain control—Use Internet filtering software and parental control guides.

Create a buddy system—Approve your child's buddy list.

Watch the Camera—Beware of and closely monitor use of it.

Webcam—Most new laptops have them built in.

Keep secure—Be aware of Web sites that don't begin with https: they are not secure.

Protecting your child in Cyberspace:

Never give out passwords—Keep passwords secret; nothing is safe on the Internet. Use password protection!

Keep personal information confidential—Social security and credit card numbers, personal addresses, phone numbers, and birth dates can be dangerous in the wrong hands. Beware of identity theft.

FREE isn't always free—Many scammers offer free things (that you will never receive) to trick people into providing information, which can then be used to steal your identity.

Don't click with just anyone—If you don't know whether an offer is from a reputable provider, don't respond.

Photo Ops—Unless it is a password-protected photo Web site you control, don't allow your child to upload and post photos anywhere in cyberspace.

Screen those screen names—It is inappropriate for children and not smart for adults to use sexually explicit screen names such as *2hot2handle@email.com*.

Never open any site you're not familiar with—It can open the door to a computer virus.

NET COURTESY

ID, please—Always identify yourself when chatting with your friends.

Type in good taste—Use appropriate language.

Extinguish all flames—Flaming is also known as slandering or engaging in hostile or insulting exchanges.

Show some sensitivity—Do not hurt other people's feelings.

Keep caps under wraps—It is equivalent to SHOUTING when you type in all caps in emails.

Spelling counts—Don't forget to spell check.

Break the chain—Never forward or believe chain letters.

Warning

Web cameras allow users to see other users in person. Sit with and monitor your child's exchanges using a webcam.

Is the V-Chip Enough?

On average, children spend four hours a day watching TV, more than any other single activity. Does your TV whine in the background through meals, homework, and even sleep? Has it become your family's security blanket?

Tip: It is your responsibility to evaluate the content of the programs your child views. Provide that information to your child's caregiver.

Research has found that TV can negatively impact your child's behavior. TV can desensitize children to violence and aggression and can become physically and emotionally addicting. On many children's shows, adults are portrayed as clueless and stupid and children's lack of respect for adults is accepted. Disrespect on TV has run rampant and this pervasive problem must be addressed by parents. Talking to children about what they see on TV gives you a chance to reinforce your Blueprint and integrate your beliefs and values.

Here is a familiar scenario... You come home from work tired and exhausted. Junior and his sister are cranky and you need to make dinner. The TV gets turned on and you go into the kitchen to prepare the meal. But did you know that these innocent looking cartoons are displaying disrespect, bullying, aggression, defiance, verbal abuse, foul language, and sexual content?

Most parents with young children know that the V-Chip helps to filter unsuitable shows that come into the home. The question is: do you use it and is it password protected?

Facts of the Manner:

The average child will watch 8,000 murders on TV before finishing elementary school.
- A.C. Nielsen Co.

According to the Centers for Disease Control (CDC) in 2008, the childhood obesity epidemic is directly related to children watching more than 1–2 hours of TV per day. ABC's *Desperate Housewives* is the most popular network broadcast TV show for ages 9–12 and it is unsuitable for children.

6.8 million children ages 2–11 were watching the 2004 Super Bowl and witnessed the infamous wardrobe malfunction!

54% of children have TVs in their bedroom and who knows how many more are watching TV on their cells, iPods, and laptops?

Children, ages 10–16, say they watch something different when they are alone than when their parents are around. Most watch MTV.
- Nielsen Ratings

TV producers create entertainment for profit, and the stations are in business to sell advertising and their sponsor's products. So your child's well-being and development as upstanding and respectful citizens are not necessarily their top priority. But it must be yours.

Children under the age of eight cannot always distinguish between real and fantasy and, therefore, have a difficult time appropriately distinguishing the content. Children often take things literally and will think the things they see on TV are true. Externalized outcomes are bullying, disregarding parental requests, defying authority, and disrespecting teachers.

Tame the Tube:

Television Time Management:
- ✓ Should never be your child's babysitter
- ✓ Stay off during mealtimes
- ✓ Eliminate background TV
- ✓ TV out of children's rooms
- ✓ Content and time restrictions
- ✓ Always leave child care provider with acceptable list of programs

Shaping your Child's Viewing Habits
- ✓ Encourage outside activities like bike riding, skating, sledding, etc.
- ✓ Set up an ongoing family jigsaw puzzle for all members to work on
- ✓ Kitchen science projects that are age appropriate
- ✓ Let your child be assistant chef for the day
- ✓ Interactive videos that encourage physical participation

And tune into:
- ✓ Planning activities with your children
- ✓ Setting clear guidelines for programming and have a list of acceptable programs for viewing
- ✓ Informing your babysitter / family members what programs are acceptable
- ✓ Family educational channels such as Animal Planet, Discovery Channel, History Channel, Cooking Channel

CHAPTER SIXTEEN

EAT, DRINK, AND BE MANNERED

Table Manner Musts

People with proper table manners make a sophisticated impression on others. These dining refinements give you an edge in the business world where deals are made over meals. You will feel self-confident and self-assured when you have mastered proper table etiquette, and nothing feels better than knowing you are comfortable around every dining table.

Reinforcing good table manners can be done at home or on the run. Napkins on the lap can be taught in a donut shop! Family dinners foster the teaching of good manners and create a ritual that stays with your child forever.

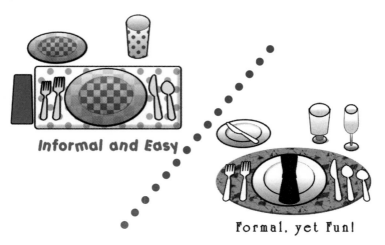

Informal and Easy

Formal, yet Fun!

BEFORE the meal, teach children to:

Scrub Up—Come to the table with hands washed and dressed appropriately. The food will look good and so will you.
Cover Up—Place napkin on the lap.
Hold Up—Wait for everyone to be seated and served before starting to eat. Having dinner together means having dinner together.
Give it Up—Come to the table without cell phones or video games.
Sit Up—Avoid tilting back in your chair. It's the best way to avoid cuisine—related concussions.
Elbows Up—Keep them off the table ... cut your risk of getting table elbow.

During the meal, teach children to:

Avoid Sneak Previews—Don't talk with food in your mouth, it's gross!
Pace your Face—Take small bites and eat slowly.
Break Bread—And butter a small piece of bread at a time.
Pass them Both—Pass salt and pepper together even if only one is requested.
Never Blow it—Don't blow on food to cool it off. It's just not cool.
Arc the Spoon—Move soup spoon away from you to eat, not toward you. Think of it as keeping your soup and spoon in sync.

Cut it Right—Slice your food servings one piece at a time. Just eat what you can. You can always take home some leftovers.

Say "No thank you"—That's the best way to turn down food you don't want ... or wouldn't eat even to win money on a game show.

Serve it Up—Use serving dish utensils to put food on your plate, not your own utensils. Ignoring this is far worse than double-dipping chips.

Exit Right—Say "May I please be excused," when you need to leave the table.

After the meal, teach children to:

Ending it—Place your fork and knife in the 4:20 position on your plate. There is a time and place for everything, including the end of a meal.

Complimenting it—Thank the person who prepared the food. This shows another kind of grace after meals.

Take it—Excuse yourself and take your plate to the kitchen. You helped eat, now please help clean up.

> **UNACCEPTABLE!** Passing gas, belching, or making inappropriate noises during dinner.
> **UNSOPHISTICATED!** Removing food from your teeth at the table.
> **UNADVISED!** Pushing your plate away from place setting.
> **UNSIGHTLY!** Using a hairbrush or a comb at the table.
> **UNREFINED!** Stacking or scraping plates when removing from the table.
> **UNTHINKABLE!** Removing plates from the table when people are still eating.
> **UNSANITARY!** Skipping the washing of your hands after using the restroom.

Pass the Peas, Please

The sooner you begin to socialize your children in restaurants, the sooner they will get accustomed to different dining experiences.

Whether you choose a fast food or four-star restaurant, you will need to know these common tips before venturing out with little ones. Remember, success at any restaurant is all about planning ahead.

Fast Food Restaurants—Manners to Go

> **Keep order**—Be patient and wait your turn to place your food request.
> **Line up your choices**—Review the menu while you wait in line and make decisions before ordering.
> **Eat without exercising**—No climbing on chairs! Children must learn the difference between an eatery and a gymnasium.

Watch what goes into and comes out of your mouth—No screaming, yelling, arguing, or clowning around.

Before you hit the road—Don't mess up a good time by forgetting to clean your own table before leaving.

Family-Friendly Restaurants—Advice that will serve you well

Where to eat—Buffets, cafeterias, and chain restaurants are all good choices.

Time to eat—Breakfast on weekends works well or an early dinner.

Prepare to eat—Call ahead to see if the restaurant has a children's menu and highchairs.

Start to eat—Ask for water and crackers as soon as you are seated.

"Always Have It With You Bag":
Extra bibs
Disinfectant wipes
Wet Ones brand wipes
Toddler fork and spoon
Crackers
Small toy

It is extremely inconsiderate and insensitive to leave a filthy mess of food under your table and chair for the waiter to clean up. Show your child that you have respect for your server by cleaning up what you can before leaving the restaurant.

—Coach Lori

CHAPTER SEVENTEEN

DIFFERENT STROKES FOR DIFFERENT FOLKS

To Make a Difference, You'll Need to Accept Differences

 As your child grows and develops, he or she will be exposed to a variety of individual differences. Children begin to notice and question these differences in people and customs early in life. Whether it is a wheelchair-bound child, someone of another color, an obese classmate, or a child with no hair, it is your ***unconditional responsibility to teach tolerance.***

Your child's success in the world will depend on understanding and appreciating individual differences. Children mirror the values and attitudes they see and learn in the home.

Here are some easy tools to teach tolerance:

- ✓ Practice tolerance in the home with patience and forgiveness.
- ✓ Always demonstrate respect for others.
- ✓ Be aware of telling stereotypical jokes and stories.
- ✓ Answer children's questions about differences openly and respectfully.
- ✓ Value the differences in your own family and point out each member's distinctive qualities.

✓ Involving your child in multicultural experiences and exposing them to cultural diversity teaches tolerance.

Many people are uncomfortable or fearful around people with disabilities. But there is no reason to be! The message that must be delivered to your child is that people with disabilities are normal and have physical limitations.

When you meet someone with special needs:

Tip: Never stare at a person with a disability. It is rude and inconsiderate. Be courteous, not condescending.

Support those who are challenged—Do not be afraid to ask if a person needs help. Wait for their response.
Keep handicap areas available—Never use a handicap bathroom stall or handicap parking spot if you are not disabled.
Announce yourself—After greeting a visually challenged individual, ask first to shake their hand.
Treating guide animals—Do not pet or disturb a guide animal.
Special equipment—Never move or touch a wheelchair or crutches without permission.
Be patient—Take extra time to be sensitive with anyone who has a speech or hearing impairment and let them know if you do not understand them.
Speak normally and directly—Avoid shouting or using a loud voice. We tend to do this, especially with foreign visitors.

The correct term to describe someone with a disability is disabled, *not* handicapped. *Only refer to a person's disability when it is appropriate and necessary.*
      —Doc Jodi and Coach Lori

Tip: When conversing with a person to describe someone with a disability, use words that are positive such as, "John is a person with a disability," or "Darren is a person who is blind."

Stereotypes: Label Clothes, Not People

Stereotypes are not only hurtful, they are also untrue. It can lead to bigotry, prejudice, and ultimately, it is disrespectful and results in discrimination.

Next time someone you're with labels a person with a stereotypical sticker, make it your responsibility to inform that person they are mistaken. If you sincerely want your children to make a difference, it begins here.

Don't believe it ... Don't accept it

Motorcycle bikers are thugs.
Folks driving pick-up trucks are rednecks.
Men with black hats and beards are terrorists.
People with turbans are fanatics.
Everyone with a southern accent is a hick.
All New Yorkers are rude and crude.
Disabled folks obviously cannot manage on their own.
Men make better doctors and women make better teachers.

Putting the Blueprint to Work: Helping Those Less Fortunate than You

A critical element in developing your family's Blueprint for Living is showing compassion to others. Here's how you—and your child—can enjoy the satisfaction that comes from demonstrating acts of kindness.

Create Feel-Good Moments

If you want your child to be a contributing member of society, decide as a family what you can do to make the world a better place.

- ✓ Have your children watch you do a good deed for your neighbor and then explain why you feel good doing it.
- ✓ Create opportunities for your children to experience helping others. Provide a list of charities and have each child choose a charity event to participate in. Example: Volunteer at your local Humane Society or Habitat for Humanity; help raise money for disadvantaged children and donate your time for their events.
- ✓ Remember that children recuperating in hospitals are so appreciative to receive donated books and toys.

Hannah, a 7-year-old, called her grandmother to tell her she cut off her long hair. When her grandmother asked why, she explained, "I grew my hair long to give it to a little girl who lost her hair from cancer."

CHAPTER EIGHTEEN

PETIQUETTE

Creature Kindness

Respect for an animal is a small part of the bigger picture of learning kindness, compassion, accountability, and responsibility. Since most children are naturally drawn to animals, having a family pet is an ideal way to increase a child's self-esteem and help children build moral character.

It is well documented that children who treat animals with kindness will, most likely, treat people with kindness. It is the parent's responsibility to teach young children that hurting a pet is like hurting a friend. Animals have feelings just like people.

Benefits of Owning a Pet:

SATISFYING—They make children feel good.
EMPOWERING—A pet will be dependent on you for care and love you for providing it.
SOOTHING—Furry friends can be therapeutic.
INVIGORATING—They make excellent exercise partners.
CALMING—Scientific studies have shown that owning a pet is beneficial as a natural stress reliever.
COMFORTING—Pets are great at cheering up a sick child.
SOLVING—A pet can be a loving companion to combat loneliness.

Parents should limit expectations for very young children. Toddlers often see a pet as an object to squeeze, tease, or even hit. To teach kindness, use a stuffed animal and role play with your child how to touch and pet it. It is also extremely important to teach your child to respect your pet's need for alone time.

Include Your Child in the Pet Care Process By:

Teaching gentleness when playing with an animal or pet.
Asking permission from the owner before touching a pet.
Creating house rules for the pet and sharing them with houseguests.
Standing back during feeding time so the animal can eat in peace.
Prohibiting teasing to ensure your pet doesn't get annoyed or angry.
Being alert to your pet's signals (growling, hissing, lip curling).
Supervising your child during feeding and cleaning up.
Being protective by not tolerating any harm toward your pet or any other animal.

Spread the Word about Pet Etiquette:

Tip: Never leave a young child alone with a pet. Animals can be unpredictable —just like young children.

COLLECT and donate pet food, blankets and accessories to your local pet shelter.
REQUEST inexpensive pet toys as part of your child's birthday gift to donate to a pet shelter.
CONSIDER asking for donated pet food at a yard sale.
SAVE someone's pet from being euthanized—offer to be a surrogate pet parent.
ADOPT an older pet from a family that had children—older animals make great pets!
TAKE your pet on family vacations. Many hotels are now pet friendly.

Pet ownership translates into compassion for others and teaches children the virtue of kindness in their own life. Owning and caring for a pet is a serious commitment that takes collective family responsibility. If you are getting a new pet, make sure the breed and temperament are a good match for the family.

—Doc Jodi and Coach Lori

CHAPTER NINETEEN

BE COOL WITH SCHOOL

The ABCs of School Etiquette

The majority of teachers today are frustrated and at their wits end because of poorly mannered children. It's all too common to see youngsters who jump out of their seats, talk back to teachers, use foul language, and other disrespectful behavior. When teachers struggle to control their classroom, well-mannered children are prohibited from learning. If children have not learned to respect authoritative figures before starting school, they will not hold their teacher in high regard.

Teachers are distracted by children who:

- ✓ Cannot keep their hands to themselves
- ✓ Tattle on others
- ✓ Call out answers without being called on
- ✓ Interrupt others
- ✓ Bully other children
- ✓ Do not follow directions
- ✓ Cannot accept constructive criticism
- ✓ Touch/take others' belongings

The number one pet peeve teachers have, outranking problems regarding testing, funding, and discipline, is *dealing with parents*. Teachers report the rampant problem of incredibly rude parents who drop small children off in the morning, or pick them up after school, while on their cell phone. Not only do these parents disregard the teacher, they do not acknowledge their child. This blatant disrespect for the teacher and the disconnection with the child sends a confusing message to both.

How your child sees *you* interact with her teacher, is how *she* will. A positive interaction sets the tone for a constructive learning environment and paves the way for open communication.

When parents develop a greater appreciation for the important role they play in their child's education, a new and much better working relationship is formed with the teacher. This relationship will help clarify what really happens in the classroom—what your child tells you vs. what the teacher reveals.

—Coach Lori

Lessons all parents should learn:

Show some class—Refrain from criticizing or disagreeing with the teacher in front of your child.
Avoid going over the teacher's head—Deal with the teacher *first* instead of going directly to the principal.
Don't be an absentee—Plan ahead and attend all parent–teacher conferences.

Do your homework—That means making sure your child does his or her homework.
Make no excuses—Never write excuses to get your child off the hook for uncompleted assignments she neglected to do.
Never be de-grading—Don't interfere with the grading process. If you have a question about your child's grade, make an appointment and discuss it.
Beat the bell—Consistently get your child to school on time.

Beware of school cafeteria concerns! Keep lines of communication open to make certain your child is eating lunch. Your child may be a victim of food bullying, someone making fun of her meal, and/or not being included to join others at the table.

Street Smarts

A Plan for Making Parents Smarter

Bedtime should be a stress-free culmination of the day. A period of quiet time is an essential prelude to falling asleep. Talk quietly with your child about the events of the next day, read a story, or give your child a massage—what a great way to end the day!

Tip: If your child feels anxious at bedtime provide a nightlight, flashlight, and her favorite stuffed animal.

P.M. Routine:

✓ Check each child's personal calendar to see what they need for the next day (i.e., tennis racket, instrument, etc.)
✓ Take clothing out

Getting to school on time can frustrate even the calmest parent. Starting the day with a positive morning attitude is critical to kicking off classroom success. Parents must establish a set of morning rules and put them into action. Make your child personally accountable for being responsible in this process. The goal is to ensure that everyone gets off to a less stressful day.

A.M. Ritual:

- ✓ Bathroom business, brush teeth and hair
- ✓ Get dressed
- ✓ Come to breakfast dressed and ready to go to school
- ✓ No TV in the morning. TV is a major distraction and only adds to the morning craziness.

Helpful activities for parents and kids to enjoy:

Construct a "Taskmaster"—Help your child create his own personal Task Chart—"The Taskmaster"—and hang it in the bathroom or his bedroom.

Play "Out to Lunchers"—Save time while cooking dinner by having your child clean out her own lunch box for the next day. Encourage an older child to make his own sandwich/snack.

Experience "Warm and Wear"—On cold days, toss your child's clothes in the dryer to make them nice and toasty warm. It's guaranteed to warm up their hearts, too.

Beat the Buzzer—Your child is less likely to sleep late if you encourage her accountability by letting her choose and set her own alarm clock.

Give Your Child a Tune Up—Allow each child to pick out a song to be played on the following morning and see which child is all dressed and ready at the breakfast table before the song ends. The winner selects the breakfast for the next day.

This scenario is all too familiar in divorced families. Your child comes home from the other parent's home missing her homework assignment and favorite bedtime stuffed animal. Your first impulse is to scream at your child and curse at the other parent's irresponsibility. Both parents must help their child pack for school to ensure a smooth transition. When both parents cooperate, children feel secure and can focus on their day.

—Doc Jodi

Driving your child to and from school can provide an essential bonding period. It allows you to "eyeball" how your child is doing and nip a potential problem in the bud. In a confined space with limited distraction you will also gain much needed undivided attention. Turn off all electronic devices and just enjoy the ride.

Carpool Rules

All carpooling parents must jointly make and agree to the following rules:

> **Pick up time**—Be ready to leave on time
> **"Chauffeur" courtesy**—Greet the driver
> **Wear a belt**—Buckle up for safety—It's the law
> **Director of directions**—The driver makes the rules
> **Rules of the road**—No fighting, screaming, or arguing
> **Stay in control**—No playing with windows, radio, or door locks

Bus Business

Before hopping on the bus, remind your child to:

> **GREET**—Say good morning to the driver
> **SEAT**—Stay seated
> **RETREAT**—Keep hands to self
> **NEAT**—Keep all belongings out of the aisle
> And keep a lid on the **HEAT**. No fighting or horseplay.

CHAPTER TWENTY

MALLS AND MOVIE MAYHEM

Managing Mall Monsters

Have you ever been in a dressing room trying on a new dress when a young child slides under the curtain playing hide and seek? Many parents bring children to the mall to entertain them, but malls are not meant to be a playground. Adults come to malls to shop and socialize. It is also a place of business for shop owners. It is extremely rude and discourteous for children to yell and tear up and down the mall walkway. It is frustrating to watch children in a store run between clothes and wipe dirty hands on walls and merchandise.

Plan your trip to the mall carefully to avoid obvious problems. Always tell your children what is expected of them and define the boundaries.

New Mall Rules:

> **Be shoppers, not zookeepers**—Running wild, swinging on store equipment, and jumping around disruptively are all behaviors that must be tamed.
>
> **Avoid doorway obstruction**—Blocking store entranceways or preventing others from entering stores with strollers or packages is rude, rude, and rude.
>
> **Don't put your child on display**—Make sure your child doesn't touch displays or get overly friendly with mannequins.

Turn on curse control—Foul and obscene language needs to be permanently shelved. So does running through the mall screaming and shouting.
End food court chaos—Be considerate of shop owners and don't bring drinks or food into stores where they can be spilled and stain the merchandise. That also goes for sticky foods on your child's face and hands.

WARNING

Keep a photo of your child in your wallet at all times.

Have an action plan with your child if she gets separated from you. Teach her to ask for help from a security guard or a clerk behind the register in a store.

For older children who are dropped off at the mall to socialize, follow these additional guidelines:

Say NO to Solo—If your child is going to socialize rather than shop, make sure he is going with friends you know and approve of.
Pre-plan it—It should be decided in advance when and where you are going to drop off and pick up your child.
"Flesh out" proper attire—Implement a proper dress code for your child and stick to it. There are lots of respectable clothes at the mall and your child should own some.
Lay down the law—Reinforce that shoplifting is illegal and punishable by law. Your child could be considered an accomplice if he or she is with someone who commits a crime.

Socializing at malls is a rite of passage. This seemingly benign outing can be much more dangerous than meets the eye. Often children will test the boundaries and act out impulsively. Older children go to the mall to "hook up," smoke, and shoplift. Most alarming, some children leave the mall without their parent's knowledge, sometimes with strangers.
—Doc Jodi

Movie Manners

Have you been to a movie lately on a Friday night? Missed any dialogue because of yapping teens or younger children crying? Have you walked out of the movie with popcorn in your hair or candy stuck to your shoe? Does your local movie theater feel like a day care center? In many major cities and small towns, patrons have been complaining about unruly and discourteous teenagers, and managers are taking action by tossing out teens who are texting and talking.

Movie Manner Guidelines

BEFORE the movies:

Pick it—Stand off to the side when you're looking at the movie listings to decide on a show or time. Why hold up the line if you're not ready?

Pay for it—Have your money, credit card, ID, or gift certificates ready before you step up to the box office.

Shut it—Don't start or take a call on your cell phone when you are paying for the ticket. Turn off your phone as you enter the theater.

112

DURING the movies:

IN PASSING—Say "excuse me" if you need to pass in front of people coming into or out of the row—especially if you step on their toes!

MOVE DOWN—If the movie is crowded, move over so that two people who came together can sit together.

FLATTEN FEET—Avoid resting your feet on top of the seat in front of you. It's not only rude, it makes for a lousy view for people behind you.

LIPS CLAMPED—Talking, throat clearing, and loud noises are all no–no's. The audience paid to hear a much more interesting soundtrack.

SNACK SILENTLY—If you're snacking, try not to make so much noise that it sounds like you're climbing into the bag or feeding the whole audience.

REPEAT THIS—"I will not repeat lines from the movie to my partner while the movie is playing." Remember, the movie theater is not your living room.

AFTER the movies:

PICK UP your garbage when the show ends and deposit it in the trash receptacle. You made the mess, why should theater personnel clean up after you?

FILE OUT by leaving the theater in an orderly fashion. There are much nicer ways to make contact with people than pushing, bumping, and banging into them.

Tip: Infants do not belong at the movies, period. If you can't get a babysitter, stay home!

CHAPTER TWENTY-ONE

TRAVEL STRAINS, DRAINS, AND PAINS

Tempering Transportation Terrors

Flight Attendant

"Welcome aboard, ladies and gentlemen. We expect lots of bumps and ulcer-causing activity on today's flight. Many children are flying with us so please prepare for countless sudden eardrum-shattering sounds and back-cracking jolts to seats. Also, watch out for debris in the aisles. It will seem to spread like poison ivy over the course of what will seem to be a very, very long flight, even though flying time will only be one hour and thirty minutes."

Have you vowed never to fly cross-country again? You and your child must be respectful of other commuters wherever and whenever you travel. If your child is whining or screaming in the plane—FIX IT! Get up, move around—do something. It's your responsibility to know how to calm your child BEFORE you get on the plane. The way you plan ahead for your trip will help everyone on board, including your family. Here are some helpful tips to keep you and other commuters sane and smiling on your journey.

Takeoff to Tranquility:

Stay calm—Use your inside voice and keep your children decompressed.
Look out!—Window seats provide additional distractions.
Ain't that a kick?—Never allow your child to kick the seat in front of him. Save the kick for karate.
No meltdowns—Don't bring snacks that melt on or stick to clothing, skin, or seats.

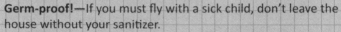

Germ-proof!—If you must fly with a sick child, don't leave the house without your sanitizer.
No one likes a crybaby—Know the right moves to calm your child down quickly, before you set foot on the plane.
Turn off your toddler's turbo engine—Never let your child run up and down the aisles.

Example

Miles keeps kicking the seat in front of him. The man sitting there keeps turning around and is becoming increasingly annoyed. Miles' dad should make Miles personally apologize to the man. This will teach Miles to take responsibility for his actions. Plus, the reality of facing the "victim" will make Miles more aware of the fact that he is disturbing someone.

Preempting Public Problems

✓ Don't push ahead in line. Wait in turn behind someone not beside someone.
✓ Hold the door open for the person behind you.
✓ Let people off before you get on.
✓ Have your money or pass ready before boarding.

In subways, buses, trains, and other public transportation, respect other's space. Turn off your cell phone, watch foul language, and speak quietly to your neighbor.

Car Travel: Put the Brakes on Non-Stop Disruptions

How many times have you threatened to stop the car... go "back there"... and @#$%^&! Probably a thousand times too many. Traveling in a car with children can be a very trying experience, mainly because you're trying to concentrate on driving while they're trying to rock your sanity.

Brake for this advice:

Load up—Plan ahead and pack the car with blankets, pillows, toys, and food before driving off.
Steer ideas—Encourage older children to contribute ideas when planning the family trip.
In the pits—Make the pit stops work for you—a fast food play area will expend energy.
Swap seats—When more than one child is in the car, alternate their seating preferences.
Wake up—Awaken children 10 minutes before arriving at your destination to give them time to adjust.

Halting Hotel Hot-Wheelers

You've finally fallen asleep at Hotel Happiness when you are awakened by shrieking, screaming kids running down the hall. Hours later there are doors slamming as late-night revelers are returning to their room. Finally, as sleep arrives at 6:00 A.M., Dora the Explorer explodes from the TV across the hall!

Parents must be responsible for supervising their children and teaching them the importance of respecting other guests.

Stop slamming—Shut hotel doors quietly.
Quit broadcasting—Turn television volume down to avoid disturbing other guests.
Stamp it out—Diffuse disruptive behavior in common hotel areas such as: hallway sprinting, lobby wrestling, elevator button pushing bingo, and towel snapping fights at the pool.

Tip: Families with young children should book reservations in a family-friendly hotel. It is unfair to everyone, including your child, to stay at a ritzy hotel if your child doesn't have ritzy manners.

INITIATING CRUISE CONTROL

Taking a cruise is meant to be a relaxing experience. But when was the last time you *really* relaxed on a cruise? Some parents bring children on a cruise and maintain a total "do what you please" attitude. Parents assume that once the ship leaves port, the responsibility falls on the ship's Activities Director. Often, guests see children running through the ship with no supervision, especially at night.

Steer Your Own Ship

Tip: Children must have a curfew on board the ship. They do not belong in adult-only activities such as an adult Jacuzzi or nightclub. Adhere to all rules while on board this out-at-sea community.

Cabin Courtesies—No doors slamming and TV blaring; no screaming or running down the hallways.

Buffet Behavior—Observe the dress code. No overstuffed plates; if your children are dining with you, prepare them in advance for what is expected of them.

Poolside Politeness—Don't be a chaise hog. It's not okay to save a dozen chairs. No belly flops that drench guests.

Showtime Sensitivity—Be on time for activities. Clean up after yourself on the ship.

Port Perspectives—At ports of call, know when to come back—or the ship will leave without you. Be respectful of the cities you visit.

It's Polite to Stair—Use the stairs when possible and save the elevators for older guests.

CHAPTER TWENTY-TWO

HONOR THY NEIGHBOR

Handling Habitat Havoc

It's 8:00 P.M. and you're just getting home from work. Worn out and exhausted, you turn into your neighborhood and feel your blood pressure rising. Once again, you spot an overturned trash can, strewn toys, and uncut grass on your neighbor's lawn. Then, to make matters worse, you step on his dog's poop! When is enough—ENOUGH?

Apartment/Condo Considerations:

Darn those annoying neighbors—Moving furniture later than 9:00 P.M., young children jumping up and down at 5 A.M., and Fido barking every hour is absolutely infuriating.

Open lines of communication by calmly and respectfully talking with your neighbor.

A space advisory—Keeping your possessions in place makes your property—and you—look better.

For your ears only—Family secrets, like jewelry, belong in the vault. Keep private matters private.

Elevate yourself—Nothing is more annoying than trying to get off the elevator when others are trampling you to get in. Let others off before you get in.

Don't sweat it—No one wants to workout on mats or equipment that's wet and sweaty. Bring your towel and have consideration for others.

Rule of thumb—30-minute use for cardio equipment, especially if someone is waiting.

Home and community awareness:

Dealing with inconsiderate neighbors—Communicate your concerns with your neighbor—don't inflame—be respectful in your message. Your goal is to resolve the issue, not create a greater problem.

Keep up your property—It's not only to keep your home's value, but also to look respectful and feel a sense of pride.

Pool Perils

Kids love the pool, but parents have to realize that it's really just a different kind of playground—in water. That means playground rules apply, but they also need to be altered because this play area has its own unique set of dangers.

Example:
Billy did a belly flop that got everyone's attention—especially Mrs. Fernandez, who got drenched and now needs to go back to the salon. Remember, it's a public pool, but that doesn't mean you have the right to drown out everyone else's fun.

Public Pool Rules

Do not drop children off at pools unattended.

> **Avoid drifting off**—Children should use water toys away from adults.
> **No one likes it**—Do not splash others in the pool.
> **Pools aren't floating bathrooms**—Do not bring babies in diapers into adult pools.
> **There's enough pool for everyone**—Instruct children to be respectful of adults exercising in the pool.
> **Take it with you**—Leave with the toys you came in with.

Private Pool Rules

How to have a big splash at your pool without it being a washout:

When invited to your neighbor's pool:

> ✓ Agree on who will watch the children.
> ✓ Always bring your own towels and suntan lotion.
> ✓ Don't assume that you are also invited to bring your friends to someone else's pool.
> ✓ Don't enter your host's home unless invited to do so.

CHAPTER TWENTY-THREE

RESPECTING OUR PLANET

Be Seen Going GREEN

It is everyone's responsibility to be accountable and responsible for our planet's survival. Faster than you can say eco-chic, respecting the environment has gone from the fringe to being a status symbol. And, we are learning every day that there is more to greening our lives than separating paper and plastic from our garbage.

Make green-over goals part of your Blueprint for Living. Here is how you can make your family more energy efficient:

- ✓ Make sure all of your faucets are shut off after using them.
- ✓ Turn the water off when you brush your teeth.
- ✓ Load up the washing machine/dishwasher before running it.
- ✓ Unplug all your appliances when not in use.
- ✓ Turn the lights off when you leave the room.
- ✓ Separate your recyclable materials—glass, paper, and plastic.
- ✓ Buy and use reusable shopping bags.
- ✓ Be really conscious about how much electricity you use.
- ✓ Reuse or repurpose items before discarding them.

Do you know...

To use recyclable grocery bags at the supermarket?
To pick up debris from the beach and discard it?
To pick up after your dog?
To complain when your favorite take-out restaurant uses Styrofoam?

That a soiled pizza box cannot be recycled?
To bring your own mug for your morning latte?
That a plastic water bottle is the worst planet offender?
That you throw away thousands of pounds of paper a year in gift wrap and tissue paper?

Facts of the Manner:

In Texas alone, 130 million cigarette butts are tossed out of car windows each year. Cigarette butts are the most littered item in the United States.

Each year the United States uses 30 billion plastic and 10 billion paper grocery bags, requiring approximately 14 million trees and 12 million barrels of oil.

Turning off your car when waiting in the carpool lane prevents greenhouse gas pollution.

If everyone in the U.S. refused to take their ATM receipts it would save a roll of paper so long it could circle the equator 15 times.

The energy we waste using bottled water is enough to power 190,000 homes.

45% of global warming pollution through vehicle emissions is contributed by the U.S.

Please visit goinggreen.com for more tips and facts.

Empower your family to make better moral and ethical decisions regarding planet conservation. Last, look in the mirror—are you doing enough to reduce your family's carbon footprint?

CHAPTER TWENTY-FOUR

PULLING IT ALL TOGETHER

- ✓ Let your actions always speak louder than your words.
- ✓ Parents are the most influential teachers children have.
- ✓ Practice makes perfect, don't expect perfect results the first time or all the time.
- ✓ Use positive reinforcement over negative criticism.
- ✓ Mutual respect is the foundation of trust from which all other behaviors evolve.
- ✓ Make a difference in someone's life every day.
- ✓ Kindness, concern, gratitude, and a smile go a LONG way.
- ✓ Success is not measured by your bank account, but rather by the positive impression you make on others.
- ✓ Most of all, remember that Good Manners are Contagious—SPREAD THE WORD AND PASS IT ON!

Our Personal Blueprint for Self-Respect:

- ✓ **Turn your life around**—Who says you can't have it all? Just DO it!
- ✓ **You can't be in control of how other people think**—But you can be in control of yourself and how you react to them.
- ✓ **Be grateful for what you have,** not what you think you are missing.
- ✓ **Prioritize from within**—You do have choices.
- ✓ **Relinquish** rigid expectations.
- ✓ **Think of the possibilities** when you live in the moment.
- ✓ **Don't underestimate** the power of sleep.
- ✓ **Reenergize** with quiet and alone time.
- ✓ **Enrich your life** with play and laughter.
- ✓ **Put a plan into action**—Balance family, work, play, wellness, fitness, and spirituality.
- ✓ **It's appealing**—How you look really does affect how you feel and how you present yourself to other people.
- ✓ **Making time** for family enjoyment is not an option—it's a MUST! It's what your children will remember when they are adults.

Jodi and Lori

INDEX